Prayer Works

True Stories of Answered Prayer

ROSEMARY ELLEN GUILEY

Unity House

Unity Village, Missouri

First Unity House Edition 1999

To receive a catalog of all Unity publications (books, cassettes, compact discs, and magazines) or to place an order, call the Customer Service Department: (816) 969-2069 or 1-800-669-0282.

The author gratefully acknowledges permission to quote from *Torch-Bearer to Light the Way: The Life of Myrtle Fillmore* by Neal Vahle.

The publisher wishes to acknowledge the editorial work of Raymond Teague, Michael Maday, Joanne Englehart; the copyediting of Kay Thomure; the proofreading of Shari Behr and Deborah Dribben; the production help of Rozanne Devine and Jane Blackwood; and the marketing efforts of Allen Liles, Jenee Meyer, and Sharon Sartin.

Cover photograph by Myra M. Cox and design by Gretchen West.

The New Revised Standard Version is used for all Bible verses unless otherwise stated.

Library of Congress Cataloging-in-Publication Data

Guiley, Rosemary.
    Prayer works / by Rosemary Ellen Guiley.
        p.   cm.
    Some stories have been previously published in Unity magazines.
    Includes bibliographical references.
    ISBN 0-87159-243-6
    1. Prayer—Unity School of Christianity.   2. Christian life—Unity School of Christianity authors.
    3. Unity School of Christianity—Doctrines.   I. Title.
    BX9890.U505G85   1998
    248.3'2'088289—DC21   97-28382
                                                                                              CIP

Canada BN 13252 9033 RT

Table of Contents

Acknowledgments

I would like to thank the many individuals at Unity School of Christianity who helped to make this book possible: Allen C. Liles, senior director of Outreach; Mary-Alice and Richard Jafolla, former directors of Silent Unity; David Smith, director of the Telephone Prayer Ministry of Silent Unity; Paulette McCann, Silent Unity administrative assistant; Carolyn Stewart, archivist of the Unity Archives; and Michael Maday, editor of Unity Books; and all those who contributed their personal stories so that others may benefit from their experiences.

Foreword

A Zen master was once asked, "How do you maintain your serenity in the face of all the pressures in your life?" He replied, "I never leave my place of meditation." He didn't mean he stayed seated all day inside his meditation room because he had a monastery to run. He meant that he never left that inner experience of meditation which he found by turning within. From that sacred space, he was able to deal with the stresses of his life.

This illustrates the real purpose of prayer and meditation. It's not the things we ask for nor even the healings we request: it's not even the peace we find while we pray and meditate, but the subsequent poise and centeredness we are able to bring into our lives and into our world.

Abraham Lincoln was supposed to have told a story of chopping down a tree. He said, "If I had eight hours to chop down a tree, I would spend the first six hours sharpening my ax." He explained that most people would rather spend the entire eight hours hacking away with a dull ax but that he would rather have a sharp one.

Prayer is very much like sharpening our ax. Prayer is spending the time to make a connection with God and raise our consciousness so that no matter what happens throughout the day, we are better equipped to handle it.

Perhaps the highest level of prayer is understood by studying the Sanskrit word *palal,* which means "judging oneself as wondrously made." Prayer, then, becomes the means by which we can become consciously aware of our divine connection and our inherent splendor.

When we pray for others, we can bring the same inner connection to them. We can raise their consciousness and help them work through the illusions of powerlessness and lack until they, too, can know how wondrous they are made. Often, healings and miracles announce the approach of this knowledge!

This is a book of healings and miracles as told by the people who experienced them and shared with Silent Unity, the international prayer ministry located at Unity Village, Missouri. It has been compiled by Rosemary Ellen Guiley, a gifted researcher and writer who has come to appreciate the power of prayer in her own life and in the lives of people everywhere.

Prayer belongs to every religion and to no religion. You can be a Christian or a Hindu, a Moslem or a Jew. Even an atheist can pray, for prayer does not depend upon belief, although belief might be the reason we sit or kneel or fall prostrate to the floor.

Prayer can take many forms, from clasped hands in a kneeling position, to closed eyes in full lotus posture, to open-eyed rapture at an object of the beloved—both sacred and mundane. Prayer is tuning to a higher vibration until the divine connection is made. Nobody owns the rights to this or knows the only way to pray.

The important thing is to keep on doing it and to know prayer works!

—Michael A. Maday
December 1997

Introduction

In 1994 I received an invitation that changed my life. It was an invitation to visit Unity Village near Lee's Summit, Missouri, to learn about Silent Unity, the prayer ministry of Unity School of Christianity. I was researching a book on the healing power of prayer.[1] I'd long been a believer in the power of prayer, and in the past I'd occasionally called the nondenominational Silent Unity Telephone Prayer Ministry to ask for prayers. But prior to my visit, I had little idea of the scope of power generated by prayers through Silent Unity.

For decades Silent Unity has worked quietly to deliver a mighty service around the world by helping millions of people through prayer. Prayer requests arrive ceaselessly, day and night, and are handled with great compassion, dedication, and attention. The range and volume of requests are astonishing. Even more astonishing are the results—the personal testimonies made voluntarily that prayers are answered. In short, prayer works.

My visit also acquainted me with the remarkable story of the founders of Unity, Charles and Myrtle Fillmore, whose eyes were opened by prayer. Their sound, affirmative philosophy has inspired millions of people to find God.

The power of prayer which I saw demonstrated in Silent Unity convinced me more than ever that prayer should be the foundation of everything that we do in life. It is the best antidote to any challenge. I have experienced firsthand the healing, transformative power of prayer in many situations. I have witnessed that power work in the lives of others.

I welcomed the opportunity to put together this book about prayer as experienced through Silent Unity. Testimonials arrive daily at Unity. Stacks of letters are read by Unity staff. Over the years some of the letters have been published with permission in Unity magazines. Now, for the first time in the history of Unity, many letters have been collected together to create a compelling picture of the power of prayer. Not only do these letters witness the power of prayer, they also witness the indomitable human spirit to overcome any obstacle.

While I was working on this book, a Unity staffer shared with me a striking dream she'd had. In the dream, she was lifted out of her body and found herself flying over the campus of Unity Village. There she beheld an angel of immense size and power stretched over the entire 1400-acre campus. Its form was of flowing energy, its colors the exquisite palette of the sunset. The angel was centered over Silent Unity. It communicated to her that not only was this area sacred space, but it also was *protected* space.[2]

As I listened to the dream, shivers of electricity ran through me. I was reminded of my impressions the first time I had visited the Silent Unity prayer room myself. The act of praying and meditating in a place builds up a tangible spiritual energy. I felt this energy quite strongly as soon as I entered the prayer room. It was the energy of millions of prayers poured out over millions of hours day and night, the constant hum of the lines of communication to the Almighty, lines that reach from the deep heart of human need to the heart of the unconditional love of God. It was the energy of pain eased by healing, compassion, and illumination. It was the energy of thanksgiving and spiritual awakening. It was the energy of joy and miracles. This accumulated energy had built up a powerful sacred and protected space.

Jesus told us that when we pray, we should enter into the chamber within the heart to seek communion with the Father. Thus, wherever we pray, we are in sacred and protected space.

This book contains more than 150 true stories about life's most stressing situations and the answers delivered through prayer. There are stories about life-and-death emergencies, broken relationships, and miraculous healings. There are stories about financial distress, depression, and loss of self-esteem. There are stories about the anxieties of daily life, such as taking crucial exams, finding jobs, and finding lost objects. In every case, as each letter writer attests, prayer is the key to spiritual restoration and redemption.

Some of the stories are published for the first time. Others have been previously published in Unity magazines.[3] All are published with permission and retain the writers' original style, grammar, and language usage. Confidentiality is assured to all those who call upon Silent Unity for prayer; for this reason, all identifying personal information has been deleted from the testimonials.

Read these incredible stories, and picture yourself in the same situations. Many of them will ring true because you *have* been there before—or perhaps you are there now. Allow these stories to touch your heart, and then take action. If you have not made prayer a regular part of your life, do so now. Make a commitment to pray daily. You, too, will quickly see that prayer makes a tremendous difference.

—Rosemary Ellen Guiley

Chapter One

The Light That Shines for You

This is the story of the magnificent power of prayer, as witnessed by Silent Unity, one of the world's largest and most popular prayer services. Silent Unity is non-denominational. It is part of Unity School of Christianity, based near Lee's Summit, Missouri, a worldwide religious organization of prayer service, education, and publishing. Millions of people of all faiths worldwide turn to Silent Unity for help and comfort through prayer. Every year the number of prayer requests increases, as more and more people experience for themselves the tangible healing and transforming power of prayer. Prayer works, and it does so in astounding ways.

Silent Unity Telephone Prayer Ministry associates serve around the clock. Many answer the prayer requests that come in by mail—nearly one million a year and rising. Others work in the Telephone Prayer Ministry day and night, answering calls—more than 1.2 million a year and rising. They handle each request with gentleness and compassion, whether it concerns a critical, life-and-death situation, a broken relationship, or a lost possession. No request is too small for prayer. God listens to the voices of all of His children. God listens, and God answers. And miracles happen.

Silent Unity is based upon two simple ideas: prayer and united prayer. "For where two or three are gathered in my name, I am there among them," said Jesus in establishing the foundation for collective prayer (Mt. 18:20). Testimonies to the mighty power of united prayer pour in to Silent Unity.

〜

From the depths of a thankful and joyous heart I want to give this testimony for the power of united prayer.

My young granddaughter was injured critically in a car accident. After five hours of surgery the doctors gave her no chance for recovery, as they later informed her parents.

When we received the message of her injury, about noon that day a very dear friend immediately called Silent Unity for your help in faith and prayer. At four o'clock that afternoon two doctors rushed into the room where the anxious family waited and announced, "We have just had a miracle!"

There is no way to express in words the thankfulness and the abiding faith that prayers do have an awesome power for instant healing. Our loved one is now almost recovered from a ruptured liver and crushed chest. Indeed, she expects to return to school soon.

—B.C., COLORADO

〜

I have prayed with you many times during the past few months. Each time I call or write, a sense of well-being overcomes me. I want to share with you the answers to my prayers:

I have prayed for a loving relationship with a man and have recently developed one.

I have prayed for my parents' health. It was found that my mother did not have cancer, and my father's operation was a success. He returned to work much sooner than we thought he could.

I have prayed for right employment. I have been offered an administrator's position in a day-care center. A fifty-fifty partnership has been offered to me without investing any money.

These have been miracles! And I know that God is the Source.

—C.K., New Jersey

∼

It is with a grateful heart that I write to thank all my friends at Unity for their prayers and encouragement. There is a history of cancer in my family. Recently, an X-ray revealed a spot on one of my lungs. A CAT scan was then recommended. I called you and we prayed. The CAT scan revealed no problem with my lung.

Even more recently, I started bleeding and had to have a cervical biopsy and other tests. Again, I called and we prayed together. All the test results were negative. I can no longer think this is a coincidence.

Thank you for being there for me. May God continue to bless you in your wonderful work.

—M.R., New York

───◦───

Unity of prayer is made in the mind and the heart. It does not matter how far "pray-ers" are geographically separated. Silent Unity works with people all over the planet and helps to unite people with each other as well as with God.

───◦───

After I received a call from relatives informing me of problems concerned with the delivery of my daughter-in-law's first baby, I called you for prayer help.

As a family we were all working with prayer for the mother-to-be and the yet unborn child. Though we were in separate towns and cities, our prayers, along with yours, helped prevent the surgery that was inevitable if the baby did not turn into the proper position for birth.

Within an hour and a half everything had changed to a normal, natural condition. No surgery was needed. The baby was born quickly and perfectly. Mother, father, and son are all well and happy. Needless to say, grandmother is thankful and grateful to Silent Unity for its words of comfort and prayers at a time when it was difficult to be poised and centered. When I hung up the phone after hearing your reassuring words calmness surrounded me, and I realized, "Thy will, not mine" is the true meaning of letting go.

—*N.L.*, CALIFORNIA

───◦───

Such blessings of miracles and healing occur every minute of the day when people turn to God and open their hearts to receive divine light. Silent Unity hears every day about the answers that manifest immediately to prayer.

I was seriously injured, sustaining a gunshot wound to the face. After being shot, I fell forward, which fortunately allowed me to continue to breathe. I was fully conscious and noticed that I could still hear, see, and think.

While waiting for the ambulance, I prayed that I would live. Then I reflected that I was hurt so badly I might die, so I prayed that the Lord would comfort my family. Having communicated those two times, I then concentrated on trying to stay alive. I did not lose consciousness until after I was in the ambulance.

Surgery was four days later. After surgery, my wife was told by the attending physician that because of the extensive swelling and damage to my tongue and palate, I probably would not speak for at least eight weeks, and then only after speech therapy. They also said that due to the seriousness of the injuries I sustained, I would probably remain in the hospital for at least three months.

Five days after surgery I was examined, and the attending physician told me to see if I could talk. To his surprise, as well as my wife's, I said (as clearly as one can with wired jaws), "Hello, L——." I was dismissed from the hospital two and one half weeks after being shot. I was told prior to leaving the hospital that at one time the doctors did not know whether or not I would survive.

We all know the answer to my improvement is the power of

prayer. Upon reflection, there is no doubt in my mind that the reason I survived is because you, along with many people like you, took time out of your day to pray for me. My wife, daughter, and son, as well as I, thank you for the prayers you offered in my behalf. God bless you.

—R.P.L., MICHIGAN

∼

I never called upon Unity for prayer that I didn't get almost immediate response. My last prayer request was for a job, and I had a job almost literally thrown into my lap. I did not even have to go out job hunting. I had a telephone call from an acquaintance asking me how I would like to have a job with a very nice concern. Of course, my answer was yes. Four days later, I went to see about it, and the employer said he was waiting for me. I'm very happy with it.

I'm so grateful to be a part of Silent Unity. I'm trying very hard to practice its teachings. It is working for me. Again, thanks to Unity for its prayers and inspiration.

—A.D., ILLINOIS

Many testimonials speak not only of immediate answers to one problem, but also of solutions to many problems that fall into place once prayers are made.

I fell ill with a severe influenza-like disease. A week later my husband became ill, and three days later he fainted in the shower and cut his face quite badly as he fell.

The day before his fall I discovered that our automobile had been stolen, and upon reporting it to the insurance company, we discovered that our coverage had expired six weeks previously. The insurance company had neglected to send renewal notices to us. After twenty years of coverage with the same company, my husband was very discouraged. So here we were sick, our automobile was stolen, and no insurance.

About that time I began to ask myself what I was doing wrong, or what I was not doing that I should be doing. The answer was swift, as I reached for a full year's unopened, unread Unity magazines and I realized how far I had strayed from God's loving care.

I telephoned a friend, who in turn called Silent Unity for us. Immediately things began to happen. A strained relationship with close friends was healed. A troubled relationship between two business colleagues was healed (although not directly prayed for). Our health began to improve. And thirty-six days after it was stolen, our automobile was recovered, with minimum damage. Part of the damage was a scrape and sizable dent on the front fender. As my husband ran his fingers over the dent to ascertain the degree of damage, the dent sprang out beneath his touch and is as smooth as new. Never will I forget the dazed and incredulous look on his face as he hurried in to tell me of it.

Undoubtedly the greatest healing has been in my having been brought back safely to the shelter of a loving Father. I wish I could express the thankfulness, happiness, and joy with which I am filled, for the good seems never-ending.

I am deeply grateful for Unity and all you have done for me, and for the love of good and true friends. I ask your continued prayers for all whom I hold dear, and for my steadfastness and single-mindedness in seeking first the kingdom of heaven.

—J.C.S., Pennsylvania

A Humble Beginning

Unity School of Christianity and its remarkable prayer service have origins that are humble and yet deeply profound. The Unity movement was founded in 1889 after a husband and wife, Charles and Myrtle Fillmore, experienced firsthand their own miracles of healing through prayer. Charles was healed of a shrunken leg, chronic pain, and impaired vision and hearing. Myrtle was healed of terminal tuberculosis and malaria. Their experiences inspired a great vision of the works that could be accomplished through prayer, especially collective prayer when many pray together. They had the faith to make their vision real. Unity was founded to further the soul's discovery of God and to plant the seeds of God, or Truth, that would flower into a higher vision of living—the development of soul qualities which make life a beautiful and helpful experience.

Health Trials

Prior to their transformations through prayer, Charles and Myrtle Fillmore lived the lives of average Midwest Americans. They had their financial ups and downs and struggled with the challenges of raising children and with the adversity of illness.

Severe health challenges had plagued them both from childhood. Myrtle was born Mary Caroline Page on August 6, 1845, in Pagetown, Ohio, to a Methodist family. (As a girl she assumed the name Myrtle.) Early on, she was instilled with the belief that she would always be an invalid with an inherited tendency toward tuberculosis and that she would probably die prematurely. During her childhood and youth, she was frail and sickly.

Myrtle attended college and became a schoolteacher. Her health worsened with bouts of tuberculosis. About thirty years of age, she followed advice to move to Denison, Texas, for its warmer and drier climate. She opened a small private school. Her social life included an informal group of young people who met to discuss philosophy and literature and to read poetry. Through this group, she met Charles Fillmore, a railroad clerk.

Charles suffered from a painful, chronic affliction. Born August 22, 1854, in St. Cloud, Minnesota, he was ten years old when he dislocated his right hip in a skating accident. The leg did not heal. Infection and complications set in.

The family summoned doctor after doctor in their efforts to help Charles. Some of the doctors performed experimental treatments that may have actually worsened his condition. Charles was subjected to crude ministrations. In one, six running sores were created on his leg; leeches were placed on them to draw out alleged poisons. Nothing helped, and Charles remained in agony.

Finally, the hip socket was destroyed. Two large tubercular abscesses developed at the top of the leg. Doctors predicted Charles would die, and many times Charles thought so himself. He survived, but his leg stopped growing. He was bedridden as an invalid for a year and still seriously ill for another year beyond that.

Charles was left with a withered leg, little sensation from hip to knee, and chronic pain. In addition, his entire right side had been adversely affected: he was deaf in his right ear and weak in vision in his right eye. From then on, Charles was forced to walk on crutches. He also wore a 4-inch, cork-and-steel extension on his shriveled leg.

Myrtle and Charles were immediately drawn to each other. Friendship and romance ensued, and they were married in Clinton, Missouri, in 1881. Charles was determined to become a successful businessman. They had two sons and moved about the Midwest to follow Charles's business fortunes in selling real estate and insurance. For a while, Charles prospered in business in Colorado. In 1884 the Fillmores moved to Kansas City, where a third son was born. Charles made a fortune ($150,000) in a real estate boom, but then fell on hard times.

Their financial straits were exacerbated by Myrtle's poor health, which required many medical expenses. Myrtle was frustrated by the inability of doctors to improve or cure her condition. She grew weary of taking medications that did no good. In fact, her health had deteriorated to the point that doctors had given her a death sentence. Her tuberculosis was complicated by malaria. They could do nothing more for her, they said. If she remained in the inhospitable climate of Kansas City, she would soon be dead.

They considered leaving for a better climate, but stayed because of a prophetic dream had by Charles. In the dream, an unseen presence spoke of another dream he'd had years before, in which he was shown Kansas City and told he had work to do there. The voice continued, "Now you are being reminded of that dream and also informed that the invisible power that has located you will continue to be with you and your appointed work."[1] That work was soon to unfold.

The Fillmores searched for anything that might help Myrtle's health. Then, one night in 1886, shortly after Charles's mysterious dream, they attended a lecture that produced a breakthrough for Myrtle and opened the way for the birth of Unity.

Myrtle's Revelation

The lecture on New Thought was given by Dr. E. B. Weeks, an eminent metaphysician whom a friend had recommended. Myrtle was looking for solutions to illness but had no inkling that the lecture would be such a life-changing event. Dr. Weeks made one statement that changed her consciousness forever: *"I am a child of God and therefore I do not inherit sickness."* The idea that Myrtle had not inherited an invalid life—and was not doomed to die prematurely—was like a divine revelation.

Myrtle suddenly saw herself in a new way in relation to God. She understood for the first time that she was a cocreator with God and that she could tap into God's great power to make changes. She threw out her medicines and began praying to bring God consciousness into every cell of her being. She prayed repeatedly throughout the day and night. She sat in a closed room with an empty chair for the Spirit of Jesus Christ. Myrtle knew that the Spirit of Jesus Christ did come to sit in the chair and to support her efforts. She also entered into a deep study of The Gospels, especially as they pertained to healing.

Two years later she was completely healed and remained vigorous for the rest of her long life.

Of her revelation, Myrtle wrote:

∾⧼⧽∾

I have made what seems to me a discovery. I was fearfully sick; I had all the ills of mind and body that I could bear. Medicine and doctors ceased to give me relief, and I was in despair, when I found practical Christianity. I took it up, and I was healed. I did most of the healing myself, because I wanted the understanding for future use. This is how I made what I call my discovery:

I was thinking about life. Life is everywhere—in worm and in man. "Then why does not the life in the worm make a body like man's?" I asked. Then I thought, "The worm has not as much sense as man." Ah! Intelligence, as well as life, is needed to make a body.

Here is the key to my discovery. Life has to be guided by intelligence in making all forms. The same law works in my own body. Life is simply a form of energy and has to be guided and directed in man's body by his intelligence. How do we communicate intelligence? By thinking and talking, of course.

Then it flashed upon me that I might talk to the life in every part of my body and have it do just what I wanted. I began to teach my body and got marvelous results.

I told the life in my liver that it was not torpid or inert, but full of vigor and energy. I told the life in my stomach that it was not weak or inefficient, but energetic, strong, and intelligent. I told the life in my abdomen that it was no longer infested with ignorant ideas of disease, put there by myself and by doctors, but that it was all athrill with the sweet, pure, wholesome energy of God. I told my limbs that they were active and strong. I told my eyes that they did not see of themselves but that they expressed the sight of Spirit, and that they were drawing on an unlimited source. I told them that they were young eyes, clear, bright eyes, because the light of God shone right through them. I told my heart that the pure love of Jesus Christ flowed in and out through its beatings and that all the world felt its joyous pulsation.

I went to all the life centers in my body and spoke words of Truth to them—words of strength and power. I asked their forgiveness for the foolish, ignorant course that I had pursued in the past, when I had condemned them and called them weak, inefficient, and diseased. I did not become discouraged at their being slow to wake up, but kept right on, both silently and aloud, declaring the words of Truth, until the organs responded. And neither did I forget to tell them that they were free, unlimited Spirit. I told them that they were no longer in bondage to the carnal mind; that they were not corruptible flesh, but centers of life and energy omnipresent.

Then I asked the Father to forgive me for taking His life into my organism and there using it so meanly. I promised Him that I would never, never again retard the free flow of that life through my mind and my body by any false word or thought; that I would always bless it and encourage it with true thoughts and words in its wise work of building up my body temple; that I would use all diligence and wisdom in telling it just what I wanted it to do.

I also saw that I was using the life of the Father in thinking thoughts and speaking words, and I became very watchful as to what I thought and said.

I did not let any worried or anxious thoughts into my mind, and I stopped speaking gossipy, frivolous, petulant, angry words. I let a little prayer go up every hour that Jesus Christ would be with me and help me to think and speak only kind, loving, true words; and I am sure that He is with me, because I am so peaceful and happy now.

I want everybody to know about this beautiful, true law, and to use it. It is not a new discovery, but when you use it and get the fruits of health and harmony, it will seem new to you, and you will feel that it is your own discovery.[2]

Myrtle experienced a strong desire to help others heal by realizing spiritual Truth. Through prayer and affirmative thinking, Myrtle helped others to achieve equally astounding results. The crippled, the blind, the ill who were treated by her often experienced miraculous, instant healing. Myrtle gained repute as a healer, and people began to seek her for help.

Charles Is Healed Through Prayer

Myrtle's self-healing especially got the attention of Charles. Despite his spiritual interests—and a desire to be free of his chronic pain—he considered himself too scientific and practical to be swept up in faith healing. Nonetheless, he could not deny that Myrtle had healed herself. He decided to try a similar but cautious approach of sitting in prayerful silence every night in order to try to get in touch with God. He was fully prepared for his efforts to fail and fully prepared to discard any beliefs in the efficacy of prayer as a result.

But something else happened: another miracle.

At first, Charles observed no changes. He persevered, somewhat grimly, and then began enjoying his prayer times. After some months had passed, Charles realized his dreams had changed. He described them as "exceedingly realistic." Furthermore, it suddenly dawned on him that God was using his dreams as a means of communication. The information Charles received in his dreams was visionary and prophetic. These mystical dreams continued for the rest of his life, providing the inspiration for much of his visionary work through Unity.

Charles also began to heal. He wrote:

∾⤳∾

When I began applying the spiritual treatment, there was for a long time slight response in the leg, but I felt better, and I found that I began to hear with the right ear. Then gradually I noticed that I had more feeling in the leg. Then as the years went by the ossified joint began to get limber, and the shrunken flesh filled out until the right leg was almost equal to the other. Then I discarded the cork-and-steel extension and wore an ordinary shoe with a double heel about an inch in height. Now the leg is almost as large as the other, the muscles are restored, and although the hip bone is not yet in the socket, I am certain that it soon will be and that I shall be made perfectly whole.

I am giving minute details of my healing because it would be considered a medical impossibility and a miracle from a religious standpoint. However I have watched the restoration year after year as I applied the power of thought, and I know it is under divine law. So I am satisfied that here is proof of a law that the mind builds the body and can restore it.[3]

Like Myrtle, Charles enjoyed a long life of health and vigor. He discarded his crutches and eventually walked with only a slight limp. For the rest of their lives, the Fillmores spent much time in prayer.

The Founding of Unity

The Fillmores had studied all religions and were particularly drawn to an offshoot of Christian Science. In 1889 they undertook study with Emma Curtis Hopkins, a teacher who had split with Mary Baker Eddy to found her own metaphysical institute in Chicago. In 1890 the Fillmores were ordained as ministers by Hopkins.

Charles founded a magazine, *Modern Thought*, in April 1889 to reach a broader, national audience. It was renamed a year later *Christian Science Thought*. The magazine was devoted to "Pure Mind Healing." Charles repudiated Spiritualism and occultism, which he said included such things as magnetism, hypnotism, mesmerism, psychometry, palmistry, and astrology. When Christian Science founder Eddy staked her claim to the exclusive use of the term *Christian Science,* the magazine was re-named *Thought* in 1891. Later the same year, Charles was inspired during prayer to rename it *Unity.* Thus Unity the organization was also born, becoming after the turn of the century Unity School of Christianity.

From its beginnings, Unity was nondenominational Christian. As the Fillmores stated in *Unity* in 1897, their teaching was not any of the religions or doctrines for-mulated by man, but gave credit to the Truth espoused in all systems. They referred to their teaching as "Practical Christianity," defining it as "the application of all the affairs of life of the doctrine of Jesus Christ."[4]

Prayer—especially group prayer—was central to their teaching. "Both Charles and Myrtle had a fantastic faith in the power of people praying together," observed James Dillet Freeman, Unity's esteemed poet laureate who joined Unity in 1929 and served as director of Silent Unity from 1971 to 1984. "They became aware that they could be united with people all over the country without being in the same room. It was a revelation that we can have everyone in the world with us in thought. The Fillmores gave people a thought, or affirmation, to hold in united prayer at an appointed hour. This insight enabled them to change the world. They had discovered Truth."[5]

The Fillmores began hosting a prayer group in their home every evening. Myrtle especially desired to see people join in group prayer. In 1890 she founded the Soci-ety of Silent Help. She invited people to join the 10 p.m. prayer time regardless of their location. The purpose of these sessions was to meditate upon the living reality of God until it became a living reality in the mind and heart. The "pray-ers" con-centrated upon prayer affirmations published in the magazine.

The Society of Silent Help was an immediate, phenomenal success. Letters poured in from people seeking relief from illness, unhappiness, and poverty. In 1891 the Fillmores changed the name of the Society of Silent Help to the Society of Silent Unity; it is now Silent Unity.

Initially, almost all the letters asked for prayers for specific health matters. Then letters requesting prayers for financial help came in, followed by requests for help for all kinds of situations.

When the telephone became more commonplace, people called in their prayer requests. The Fillmores often took many of the calls themselves. With calls coming in day and night from all over, the telephone prayer service became an around-the-clock operation prior to World War I. Eventually, toll-free lines were added. The prayer service grew steadily over the years.

Both Charles and Myrtle worked long hours to build Unity and bring Truth to millions of people eager for a closer relationship with God. They exhibited a genuine love for their fellow human beings and personally answered many of the calls and letters for prayer.

Initially, Unity was headquartered in Kansas City. The Fillmores acquired 1400 acres of serene countryside near Lee's Summit, Missouri. There, a Mediterranean-style campus was built, with chapels, housing, administrative and educational facilities—and the Silent Unity prayer room.

Myrtle Fillmore died peacefully at home on the evening of October 6, 1931, about six months after she and Charles celebrated their golden wedding anniversary. She set a superb example of conscious dying. She chose her own time to go, cheerfully announcing to family and friends several weeks prior to her death that soon she would be leaving. She was in good health and full of vitality and could not be persuaded to change her mind. Instead, she seemed to be radiant with a vision of greater work to do on the other side. She worked at her office right up to the day before she died.

For the next sixteen years, Charles continued the work that he and Myrtle had begun. On December 31, 1933, he married Cora G. Dedrick, who had worked for the Fillmores for many years as their private secretary and had also served as director of Silent Unity.

Charles kept an incredible schedule that would have exhausted people half his age. He traveled, lectured, and gave radio talks, thriving on a few hours of sleep a night. He used affirmations as fuel to accomplish a formidable agenda. A few months before his death, he was energized by this affirmation: "I fairly sizzle with zeal and enthusiasm and spring forth with a mighty faith to do the things that ought to be done by me."[6]

In February of 1948, he became ill and his robust health faded. He was bedridden for several months before passing peacefully on July 5, 1948, at age 93. In his last months, Charles was aware that death was near, but was not afraid. His final days were brightened by a recurring vision of the New Jerusalem, the new world he had sought to create. In his last moments, he awakened from sleep and smiled, as though he recognized someone. Perhaps it was Myrtle, returning to lovingly help him in his transition. He then closed his eyes and left this plane of consciousness.

Charles took opportunities to teach others right up to the end. Once he reminded a friend that the most important words in the world are "Christ in you, the hope of glory."[7]

Silent Unity Today

Silent Unity stands as both a literal and spiritual beacon of light, illuminating the darkness of troubled minds and troubled times. Its Prayer Vigil Chapel is topped by a pleasant cupola from which lights burn 24 hours a day. "The light that shines for you" is the motto of Silent Unity known around the world.

In this month's Daily Word *is a photo of the Silent Unity window at night with the caption, "The Light that Shines for You." Years ago I visited Unity Village and bought a postcard with that picture on it.*

At that time I was just beginning to recover from alcoholism and withdrawing from prescription drugs. In the weeks to come, I was to go through the hallucinations and psychosis that often accompany that long trip back. All that time I kept your card on the wall, a beacon of hope and trust that a "power greater than myself" could restore me to sanity as the AA program promised.

Over the next couple of years, I kept your picture in sight and called you many times as I slowly regained my ability to think clearly, recovered my emotional peace of mind, and began to rebuild my shattered life.

I have been sober for 11 years. From a helpless alcoholic in and out of mental hospitals, I have become a responsible, loving parent, a caring wife, and a competent professional. In the creative work I do, I use my mind to its fullest capacity—and I have a mind to use!—thanks to you, God, and AA.

AA has told me, "There is One who has all power—that One is God. May you find Him now!" You made that possible for me. While I couldn't believe in or trust the remote God of my childhood, the ever-present, all-loving God you introduced me to has healed me totally.

Grateful seems a bland and puny word to express the deep and total joy and awe that I feel at God's work in my life. Thank you for being the instrument of His peace. Thank you for being!

—J.P., CALIFORNIA

Through prayer, the sick and injured are healed and the lonely are comforted. Silent Unity helps many to discover the power of prayer.

What would I ever do without the knowledge that I can pick up the telephone and talk to you! I have called many times and each time I have found a quietness which affects my entire body, allowing fear to subside and the life currents to work for me—then healing.

I called and told you about my son who had a piece of metal pierce the retina of his eye. He thought very little of it until the eye began to pain him, and when he saw a specialist he was informed that the eye had become seriously infected and that he might lose sight in it.

When I heard he was in the hospital, I telephoned Silent Unity. I was crying at the time, but when I hung up the phone I knew that I had done the very best thing I could for my son—turn him over to God and the prayers of Silent Unity.

The eye improved so surgery was not necessary. My son can now see out of the eye and there is no doubt in my mind that the healing is accomplished.

Unity has become my family and you have always been there

when I needed to feel God's love. Thank you for all the good you are doing for me, mine, and the world. Bless your light which continues to beckon all of us to a higher understanding of ourselves and our fellowman.

—R.S., VIRGINIA

～

One night I felt so sick and weak and lonely. I was frightened at the thought that in the middle of the night there was no one whom I could call on for help. I prayed as I always do, but gasping for breath and frightened, how could I relax and know that "closer is He than breathing, and nearer than hands and feet"?

I sat up in bed thinking, Who can I call on? My doctor is not available in the city; friends are too far away—they couldn't help me anyway. Then I remembered the light that shines for me in Silent Unity. I reached for the telephone and called long distance to you in Silent Unity. The friendly reassuring voice at the end of the line calmed my fears, and I began to feel that I was not alone after all; God's love was real and was in the warmth of the voice of real friends like you who know how to pray.

After I received the brief treatment on the phone, I went back to bed and fell asleep. The next day I felt better and continued to feel better each day. I was able to go to work. Thank God, thank you!

Yes, peace, strength, courage, faith, healing came as the answer to prayer, because you prayed with me. God bless you abundantly. Please find enclosed my love offering. You are a blessing.

—E.L., CALIFORNIA

More than 100 people staff the Telephone Prayer Ministry. They come from all walks of life and all types of professional backgrounds. They are specially trained for this demanding job, which involves a shifting kaleidoscope of prayer requests minute by minute. Callers receive prayers while on the line.

Additional staffers read prayer requests made by mail. Every letter that comes in is blessed as it is handled. Whether by phone or mail, all persons who give their name and address receive replies by mail. In addition, all prayer requests are prayed over for thirty days in the Prayer Vigil Chapel.

The staffers do not give out their names, and callers cannot request a particular staffer. This anonymity keeps the emphasis on prayer and not on personality. Myrtle felt strongly about anonymity. In the early days of the Society for Silent Help, a small group of healers were trained to handle the prayer requests. Understandably, people developed favorites and asked for specific persons. Myrtle advised them to focus instead on the Spirit of Truth, allowing it to lead them to all Truth. She said that better results are obtained when healing is done from an impersonal standpoint.

Although prayer shows us that our needs can be met, ultimately it shows us that God is within all people. Rather than seeing God as an intervenor who can help us have what we want, we begin to see God as what we want. This is a core teaching of Jesus: "And do not keep striving for what you are to eat and what you are to drink, and do not keep worrying. For it is the nations of the world that strive after all these things, and your Father knows that you need them. Instead, strive for his kingdom, and these things will be given to you as well" (Lk. 12:29-31).

Time and time again, this lesson reveals itself to those who contact Silent Unity. They call to pray for one particular thing, only to discover that when they shift their priority from things to God, a wealth of abundance opens up.

Words fail when I attempt to describe the great spiritual change which has so quietly come over all of us in the past nine months. There is today no groping. I walk with confidence in the Father's guidance, and the knowledge that perfect health and perfect peace are mine now, because I am at-one with the Father within me. I realize now that as I appreciate and use with a thankful heart the abundance of good things at hand, more is always coming. This restful love attitude influences everyone and everything, and I see evidences of its quiet constructive work constantly bringing decided changes.

—*M.S.,* Canada

I take this opportunity to express my heartfelt gratitude for the benefit I have received from your treatments. My health has improved. I feel that I have been healed of the headaches from which I suffered so terribly.

I have improved spiritually. My home is filled with peace and harmony and plenty; whereas, before there was continual discord. My two sons are converted and have made a wonderful change in their attitude in regard to home affairs. My daughter has changed greatly in disposition and in health. I have no words to express my thanks to God and to you.

—*J.E.R.,* California

∽

I wanted to let you know what has happened to me since I came to the realization that God was within me instead of in the sky. I now am able to walk without dragging my left leg. I can now hang my own wash and can reach overhead; can cut my own food; talk so people can understand me—and cook meals for more than myself and my husband. I now have a true zest for living. I have the full use of my left hand and I can make my bed when I change the sheets. Just think, I had to have all these things done for me for seven years!

I feel reborn! I keep remembering these words: "Seek his kingdom, and these things shall be yours as well."

—A.W.T., CALIFORNIA

Silent Unity works in partnership with people to help realize the kingdom of God within. James Dillet Freeman likened Silent Unity to a guide in climbing a mountain: "You might not be able to climb the mountain alone, but with a guide, united to others, you can. Silent Unity enables you to come closer to God. God is the answer, and the only place you can find Him is within. God is accessible through prayer, changing your heart, doing your very best to unite with Him, and letting God use you as a vessel of love, wisdom, truth, beauty, and joy."[8]

A call to Silent Unity is an act of prayer, a reaching out toward God that sets in motion powerful forces. First, there is an immediate feeling of calm and comfort as the troubling matter is turned over to God. As the answer to prayer manifests, a door to Truth opens. We realize that prayer is more than an answer to a question or a problem; it is the beginning of a deeper spirituality.

I phoned you with a great healing need. I was in tears and desperate to hear some comforting, reassuring words from you, which I did. All signs pointed to cancer.

I'm the only parent my two sons have, and I decided I had to live and be well again. I knew it was possible. I believed in healing, though I was afraid, knowing the severity of my condition. I thought about phoning you, and a friend urged me to do it. That soft, reassuring voice from Silent Unity got me started with my healing work. I asked for prayer support everywhere. I read and studied books on healing, and I prayed. I felt myself getting a bit stronger and had a little less pain, but the big turning point came when I went to the hospital for more ultrasound tests. The previous test had revealed an enlarged ovary with a large cyst. The doctor did not like the look of either and was preparing me for surgery and the possibility of malignancy. The ultrasound that was done prior to scheduling surgery revealed a normal-sized ovary and no cyst. The technician and doctor couldn't explain it. The cyst was miraculously gone. All was well. I was healed. All reports that followed went in a new direction—conditions clearing up, other conditions that could be treated, and the diagnosis changed from cancer to a hormone imbalance and a treatable condition—all of which I know will heal.

I wanted to share my wonderful news with you and thank you for your love and help and prayer support. It is always a help to know you are there.

P.S. I can add a postscript to my letter in that since I wrote it,

I have become one hundred percent strong once again, and am living a happier, healthier life than ever before. This is so because, through the experience of my illness, I have reached a high plane of living. I approach daily living much differently now and am benefited by attracting good from all directions into my life. My children and I are blessed each day.

—C.M., NEW JERSEY

~

Several weeks ago I wrote to you for prayers at the urging of my mother. My eyes were failing rapidly and glasses and treatments helped but very little. Along with my losing my hair this had made me desperate. Being only twenty-two years of age, I could see nothing but many unhappy days ahead. With heartfelt gratitude I can now report that my eyes are steadily improving and that my hair has ceased falling and is filled with new life, beauty, and luxuriance. In fact I am undergoing a complete change. To feel and experience the presence of God is truly wonderful. God bless you all.

—W.A.N., CALIFORNIA

~

As I look back over the past twelve or so years since I first heard of Unity, I realize that you have been a steadfast reminder to me that underneath are "the everlasting arms."

I came from a broken home, was a battered child, had an alcoholic mother, and have had quite a time overcoming those handicaps, which are just as limiting, I feel, as would be any other kind of handicap. But with your help, through Silent Unity and your publications, I am learning that I am a child of God and did not cause (by a lack in me) all those horrible things that happened to me as a child. At the same time, I have learned that I am responsible for myself and that I can, by turning to God and with His help, change anything that I want to change.

I have suffered for years with anxiety attacks, and many nights, through my fear and panic, I have remembered that just a reach away was the telephone to Silent Unity, and that knowledge has comforted me and allowed me to keep on keeping on. I am even learning to smile through my pain and fear knowing that the reality of me is not pain, fear, or difficulty.

I am enclosing a small gift which represents my sincere thanks for all that Unity has done for me through the years.

—P.M., CONNECTICUT

These testimonials are spoken from the heart. None are solicited; people simply feel moved to tell their stories. Can you feel the power of prayer behind them? Not only does prayer answer needs, it brings the glorious light of God into every facet of life. Prayer changes you at the core of your being. It opens the way to miracles.

You can experience the same blessings yourself. Is there something in your life that needs healing? That needs a change for the better? The very first step is so easy: Turn to God in prayer. Ask Silent Unity to help you by praying with you.

Chapter Two

In the Twinkling of an Eye

The most stunning evidence of the power of prayer happens daily at Silent Unity through the requests for help in emergencies. In the moment prayer is conceived and made, powerful forces go to work. Life-changing and life-saving results can occur in the twinkling of an eye. Charles Fillmore said that speedy answers to prayer are always experienced "when the right relations are established between the mind of the one who prays and the spiritual realm."[1]

Our "right relations" are made of love and a sincere desire for God's good.

Many of the calls made to Silent Unity are for medical emergencies in which life hangs in the balance in a breath and a heartbeat.

─────※─────

Recently I called for prayers for our little three-and-a-half-year-old nephew who was run over by a car. He was pinned under the vehicle for ten minutes by a hot exhaust pipe. He was in the hospital for just two days, for his only injuries were burns about the neck and chest and a "goose egg" on his little head. His recovery has been excellent! How grateful we all are!

Thank you for helping us to remove our fear and to let God's love and healing flow in.

—*M.K.*, New York

⁓

Here is a small donation to express my appreciation for the prayers offered for my grandson. Shortly before I called you, he had been rushed to the hospital after drinking kerosene. By the time he arrived at the hospital, he was much improved. His lungs, which were our greatest concern, were clear. His mouth did not show signs of damage, and he has completely recuperated.

If one could have seen him gasping for breath, catatonic and listless, just a few short minutes before I called you, it would be impossible not to see the hand of God touching our baby.

Thank you for being there!

—*C.A.*, Pennsylvania

Prayer helps us to establish our "right relations" with God. The healing power that flows can be instantaneous.

I want to express my gratitude for your prayers in a time of need, and to share with you the happy results.

I called the Silent Unity prayer room and asked for prayers for my friend who had been hospitalized with menfitas, which is a condition that precedes spinal meningitis.

She had been hospitalized for three days at the time, and up to that point her condition had continued to grow worse. When I left her bedside that night, I felt that she was very near death.

Shortly after leaving the hospital, I was talking to a close friend about the seriousness of my friend's condition. He reminded me that there was something we could do to help. That is when the thought occurred to me to call Silent Unity. Thank God I did! Thank God you were there!

The following morning I called my friend at the hospital. When she answered the phone she sounded as if she had never been sick. Just a few hours earlier she was only able to utter a few words under her breath, and didn't have the strength to open her eyes. Miraculously overnight she was transformed by God's healing grace back to the happy, healthy being that she was meant to be.

She recovered so suddenly that they kept her two extra days just for observation. She had an opportunity to thank the doctor for all he had done. He gave all credit to God and reminded her that he was only acting as his Father's instrument.

It is so good to have her well and to have friends like you who care enough to help in a time of need. God bless you.

—J.C.S., CALIFORNIA

～

During the past two months fate has necessitated our need to turn to Silent Unity with prayer requests for different members of our family and our friends who were in hospitals in intensive care (one with failing eyesight after a cataract operation; one with six inches of a malignant transverse colon removed; one having had a serious gall bladder operation; and the fourth with heart surgery).

Almost within moments after our prayer request by telephone to Silent Unity, each patient experienced a miraculous recovery and feeling of well-being. None was aware of the call made in his behalf. Each of their doctors was astounded and puzzled.

All of these persons are back at business again and have received a bonus of feeling stronger than ever before.

Our gratitude knows no bounds, and mere words are futile in trying to express it to our God and Silent Unity. We bless you, we love you, we appreciate you.

—D.E.J., FLORIDA

When crisis strikes, we are immediately thrown into turmoil, shock, anxiety, and panic. A moment of prayer turns the situation completely around: we are flooded with calm and peace and the knowledge that the divine love of God is surrounding all concerned. Silent Unity provides a vital lifeline to the peace and love of God.

I've always read in awe the letters people send telling of the miracles that have occurred as a result of prayer. Joyously, I too am writing to let you know the outcome of a tragedy in my family.

Last month my brother was in an accident, which resulted in a large hematoma requiring immediate brain surgery. He slipped into a coma and was not expected to live. I was devastated, and the only thing I could think of was to find a chapel in the hospital and pray.

As I was sitting in the chapel, I remembered Silent Unity, and wanted to call asking for prayer. I remembered that my Daily Word *was in my purse and asked my husband if he would call for me because I felt I wouldn't be able to stop crying long enough to get the words out.*

After speaking and praying with a woman from Silent Unity, my husband shared what the woman had said to him. She had told him that my brother was already better, that God was with him. At that instant, I knew in my heart that he'd be okay.

Today my brother is walking, talking, joking, and progressing at a remarkable pace. We're expecting a full recovery. This has truly been a miracle. I thank God and Silent Unity from the depths of my heart!

—*P.K.,* Minnesota

∼

Some time ago I phoned, asking for your prayers along with mine for my grandson. He was on his honeymoon and had an accident. He was scuba diving, came up under a boat and the propeller caught him on the left side of his head and face. He was taken to a hospital there. I am grateful and thankful to tell you this young man has had a perfect healing—his eye, head, and face without scars.

At the time of this injury, he was to take his law examination. He and the family were concerned. Could he study for this examination? I had asked for your prayers for this, too. Well, he was able to take his examination and was successful with excellent grades!

Thank you for your prayers, the loving voice and assurance of healing when I phoned. Thank you too, for the lovely letter and affirmation I received.

My daughter (the mother of this young man) and I had faith, knowing he would be healed. We are students of Unity, and I attend a local Unity church.

My daughter sent a love offering to help in your far-reaching wonderful work, and I am now enclosing a small love offering.

God bless each of you, and thank you again for your prayers.

—L.B., OHIO

∿

I recently called for prayers for my dearest friend. Her medical condition was grave—she had two aneurysms, and one of them had ruptured. She had a fifty-fifty chance of surviving the surgery. If she did survive, she would require months of therapy and a lengthy stay in intensive care.

The woman who took my call was so sensitive to the situation. As we prayed together, we affirmed the truth that my friend was a *child of God, enfolded in God's perfect, healing light. A sense of peace came over me, and I knew all would be well.*

I am pleased to tell you that the surgery was a success. There was no long stay in intensive care, and she was released only nine days after the surgery! There was no damage to the brain and no therapy required.

My friend frequently tells me how she can actually feel God's presence and the love of all those praying for her. Thanks to all of you for your continuing love and prayers.

—J.A., CALIFORNIA

～

Recently we called you asking for prayer for our nephew who was dying of leukemia. He was bleeding to death and the doctors were unable to stop the bleeding. The hospital was running out of his type of blood.

After you prayed with me I was confident that he would improve, and the very next morning the bleeding stopped. His doctor called it a miracle. Specialists that came in from out of town to check him over just couldn't believe his healing.

Yesterday we received a report of his latest bone marrow test. The doctors thought they surely had made a mistake, for it showed complete remission. They are doing another test as they just can't believe it. We do; we expected just such results.

May God bless you in your wonderful work.

—D.S.B., KANSAS

Our first response in a crisis is to summon help. We should be ever mindful that summoning divine help is essential too.

∿

I was caring for my little seven-month-old adopted grandchild. For several days she had been a little cross—quite unlike her usual gentle, sweet nature. When she awoke from her nap she was very lethargic and had a very high temperature.

I called her mother who was at work, and also her pediatrician. The baby was rushed to the doctor's office and then to a hospital. By that time she was nearly unconscious and her temperature had risen to an alarming degree.

While I waited at the phone for news of her condition, I thanked God for her and asked His blessings on her.

The report from the hospital was devastating. She appeared to have meningitis. There was fluid in her head and the spinal tests were extremely alarming.

I just stayed at the phone and called Silent Unity, requesting prayers for her. The lady who spoke with me had the voice of an angel. I burst into tears of gratitude. When I dried my eyes I just sat back and thanked God for Unity. The whole burden seemed to be lifted from me and I knew the child would be all right.

For three days her fever continued dropping a little and then it would go up again. Suddenly her fever dropped to normal. She woke up smiling and reaching to be held.

I received another miracle from God through the prayers of you wonderful people. My gratitude to you and to our God is unending.

Our child is fine and has no apparent after-effects of the illness. Thank you for being a part of our miracle.

—R.W.W., CALIFORNIA

∼

My sister-in-law phoned to tell us my brother-in-law was dying. He was in the hospital for heart surgery. His kidneys had ceased to function, his temperature was very high, and his blood pressure was extremely low. The doctors had told her to call the family together.

As soon as she hung up, I phoned you. Two hours later, she called to say he was getting better. He continued to improve, and five days later was on the plane coming home. I know beyond the shadow of a doubt that it was your prayers that did it.

Thank God and bless you all.

—R.K., OREGON

∼

When my granddaughter was only sixteen months old, a car backed over her head, and she was taken to a hospital. My wife immediately dialed Silent Unity for a prayer. When we arrived at the hospital the next day, instead of her being in her bed, our granddaughter was taking a walk down the hall. She ran to us and hugged us. Although she had a skull fracture and there were tire marks on her face, she was very much alive. My grand-daughter is now a healthy and intelligent seven-year-old. We are all extremely grateful for her miracle.

—P.S.W., CALIFORNIA

Prayer wields power in the face of odds that seem to be impossible and overwhelming. Myrtle Fillmore said that when we discover that prayer indeed works, we feel as though we have stumbled onto a great secret. Sometimes we discover this secret out of desperation; we feel there is nothing else we can do. We pray because it seems to be the only and last hope, because others have given up.

I called your Prayer Room and asked for your prayers for a friend. At that time his condition was very grave. He was bleeding internally; his liver and kidneys had failed to function. He was on a respirator and ultimately received forty-seven pints of blood. The doctor told his wife to call the family together because he would not survive the night.

That is when I called Unity—wonderful Unity! His condition improved so much they took him out of intensive care. He stopped hemorrhaging, his kidneys and liver started functioning again, and there was no further need for the respirator.

The doctors frankly admit that they have no explanation for his recovery, because they said he was practically dead.

My friend is doing very well, healing beautifully, is in good spirits, and we're playing golf next week! What a wonderful example of God's healing and the power of prayer.

I am very grateful for all of the help from my friends at Unity.

—R.B.O., Michigan

∼

This thank-you is long overdue. Thanks just does not seem to say all that we feel.

Christmas time was everything but a happy one for our family. Our 2-½ year old son was hospitalized with pneumonia, seizures, asthma, and encephalitis. He almost died just before Christmas. He was in ICU for two weeks and in the hospital a total of three weeks. A friend called Unity. I know all the prayers gave us the strength for our family to carry on.

The doctors did not give us much hope. Our previously active, happy and playful son was now blind, possibly deaf, could not sit up, feed himself, nor even hold up his head.

However, as each day passed he made remarkable progress. Now three months later he's alive and almost back to his "old self." He had two months of intensive therapy; but everyone feels his recovery is unbelievable. We call it a miracle.

—R.F., Nevada

∼

I am writing this letter in reference to a call I made to you a week ago Friday concerning my sister. I was told by the doctor that she had only two to five days to live. The family was told that the only thing they could do was to make her as comfortable as possible until the end. Her only hope was the Great Doctor.

Prayer and faith in God is a wonderful thing, because at some time between Saturday night and Sunday morning, with God's blessings and helping hand, the life-supporting oxygen tube that she'd depended on for so long fell from her nostrils. She didn't need it any longer. She tried to describe the feeling that came over her. But it was something that couldn't be put into words.

Sunday, it was as though a miracle had taken place. With God's good grace she got better. Monday, when the doctor came to check on her, he was amazed. Even he wanted to know what had happened. She replied that it was God's working hand. Tuesday, she was scheduled to go home, for she was still on that wonderful road of recovery. Wednesday, the Great Doctor spread His blessings, and the hospital released her. She came home. Because, there was nothing more the hospital or medical doctors could do for her.

She's at home now, up and stirring around. Her trust and faith in God and your prayers have taken her a long, long way. And we all feel that the power of God is being revealed.

To all of you at Unity, God bless you and keep your good work and prayers going. Your faith in God is superb.

—G.M., INDIANA

～

My nephew took sleeping pills and fell into a deep coma. The doctors could not predict whether he would live or die and could only suggest that we pray for him.

On the second day of the coma, I called Silent Unity, reported what had happened, and asked for prayers for my nephew. I was terribly distraught and could hardly talk. The gentleman on the other end of the phone was very understanding and compassionate and assured me that Silent Unity was with me and would pray for my nephew for thirty days. After speaking to Silent Unity, I knew deep within my heart that my nephew would be okay.

I am very happy to be able to say that on the third day my nephew started moving and on the fifth day he opened his eyes. There was no brain damage and except for a slight case of pneumonia on his right side, he is doing fine. The doctors say he should be out of the hospital within a couple of weeks.

This experience assures me that our Creator never fails.

—R.A., New York

⁓

I wanted to write to thank you for your prayers for my son. I called for help and God answered my prayers. I'm a strong believer in prayer.

My son was hit in the head by the side mirror on a truck. It cracked his skull. After surgery the doctors told me he didn't have a chance and if by any miracle he did live, he would have no mental capabilities. Well, while I was deciding that it would be better that he would die rather than live only in his physical body, something in my head said no, you keep him alive now and the rest will follow. I took his sneakers in ICU and told the doctors I was putting them on him and we would walk out of here. Of course they all thought I was crazy. But I stayed right next to him and talked and prayed and held his hand. I prayed for energy to heal him and heal his brain. Also, many prayer groups were asked to pray for him, and I believe that all that combined energy saved him. He finally came out of the coma. I was told he would be blind, have no short- or long-term memory, and would probably never function normally.

It has been over two years since the accident and he is back in school (on the honor roll). He had to learn how to walk and talk since he was paralyzed on the left side. He's not running yet, but he will. His memory is excellent. The doctors say they don't know where it all came from, but I do.

He still doesn't have the use of his left arm and hand, although we won't give up. At times he was depressed, but your prayers have helped. He seems to be back to his happy self and he says he's feeling great.

—*D.P.,* Delaware

As the previous letters demonstrate, people often determinedly pray in faith and trust in God in spite of skepticism from others. Sometimes the results of prayer do not appear within moments. Results may take days, weeks, even months or years to manifest. The passage of time in a crisis seems to slow to a painful crawl. It becomes easy to doubt whether or not our prayers will be answered as we hope. During these times, it is essential to keep praying. The power of God is at work in ways unseen.

∼

Six months ago, my ten-year-old son was struck by a car as he was crossing the street after a football game. He lay in critical condition for two weeks in intensive care and then in a coma for six weeks before regaining consciousness. Although he sustained a severe head injury, today he is back playing summer league baseball, recently earned another "belt" in his karate class, and is back in school. He lost one grade this year because of his illness and does struggle with some problems with learning. However, his recovery has been miraculous.

—J.M., LOUISIANA

∼

I have called you many times since my husband was in a very serious auto accident. As a result of the accident, he was in a coma for three weeks.

The doctors gave him no hope for surviving the first week. After he had lived through the first week, they said if he continued to live he would be a vegetable the rest of his life.

He had all the complications imaginable—a collapsed lung, double pneumonia, abscesses on the lungs, liver problems, and a very high temperature.

How God proved the doctors wrong. Through your prayers and the prayers of many friends, family, and people from churches, he has done more than just live. He is on a slow road to complete recovery. He knows people and what they are saying, and he is beginning to walk with physical therapy. It's all slow, but praise God he is alive and coming back to us.

I will continue to pray and thank God for more recovery. The doctors and nurses have had to admit it is a miracle.

I just want to thank you for your prayers and your calming presence. I call you just because hearing you on the phone calms me and fills me with strength.

—*K.W.,* California

We are often tested in our ability to hold on to the faith that our prayers are heard. It can be hard for us to do it alone. We feel as though the whole world has withdrawn and our personal reality is changing beyond our control. That fear is an illusion. The Bible tells us that God is always present, and we are never alone: "If I take the wings of the morning and settle at the farthest limits of the sea, even there your hand shall lead me, and your right hand shall hold me fast" (Ps. 139:9-10). God dwells within the heart. Prayer reaffirms that constant presence of God.

I called you for my grandson who fell sixty feet off a cliff and was in a coma for many weeks. The doctors said he couldn't live, as he had a concussion, many broken bones, and cuts; but we kept our faith knowing that God would heal him. We certainly thank God for that wonderful healing. He is being given therapy, as his leg was broken as well as his arms. He is very alert now and can talk. He will be going home soon.

God bless all you wonderful people in Unity who prayed for him.

—R.P., California

∼

We called you for prayers for our seventeen-year-old son who was in an accident and was facing brain surgery the next day. He had surgery twice in two weeks.

We are grateful for the power of prayer and God's perfect healing in our son. It has been two months now since the accident, and our son is back at work. Before school was out he was able to attend the installation of school officers and was installed as president of the student body. It was truly a day of rejoicing for all his family, his fellow students, and faculty. He expressed life to everyone, and that life is God. We feel God has great plans in store for him.

During this period of our lives, we encountered many beautiful people who expressed their belief and love for God openly, and there was great rejoicing. For this we are thankful. You have our prayers and blessings in your ministry.

—P.L., Colorado

~

I must report the miraculous outcome of the case of a little girl for whom I asked you to pray. She was hit by a motorcycle while she was returning home from school and sustained very serious head injuries. For 48 hours the doctors held no hope for her survival. She was alive, but she had not regained consciousness. A large section of her skull had been removed to allow her brain to expand, and the doctors predicted brain damage and paralysis on her left side. Her family and friends prayed for her, and I called you for healing prayers. Within a week she opened her eyes and recognized her mother. Before long she was up in a wheelchair, and soon she was on her feet walking. The piece of skull bone was able to be replaced two months earlier than at first projected, and by the middle of summer she was at her family's cottage playing and even going in the water. She is now back at school. There is no sign of paralysis, speech impediment, or memory loss! She is even taking her piano lessons as usual. Her doctor told her parents that there is no medical explanation for her recovery. He says she is a miracle child! Praise God for the power of prayer!

—J.C., CANADA

Everything has a purpose in life, even crises and tragedies. Sometimes it takes a crisis to awaken us to the power of prayer.

For some time I have received material from you, read the Daily Word, *and contributed as often as I can. I am so grateful to you and your organization.*

I felt the desire to write and let you know how Unity has influenced my life. Actually, it began before I was aware that Unity existed. Three years ago my 21-year-old son was in an intensive care unit of a local hospital. His doctors told us he could not live through the night.

I went to the telephone in the waiting room and called a friend, a very spiritual person. She said that she was going to call Unity and begin prayer treatment for my son.

We waited throughout the night for the news that we feared, but no call came. Early the next morning we hurried to the hospital. The doctor came from the room where my son had been and said, "Your son is not in there." My heart sank. Then he continued, "He is no longer in intensive care; he is back in his room." The next words from the doctor were, "Do you believe in miracles? We have no explanation for his recovery. We felt that if he survived he would have a long and gradual recovery. But for such a rapid turnaround we have absolutely no explanation."

Later my friend explained to me a little about Silent Unity and the prayer service.

Once my son came through that night so miraculously, the doctors told him that he could never walk again. My son refused to accept their opinion. In a few weeks he was on crutches, and in another few days he was walking unaided. A few days ago I stood on my porch and watched as he mowed my lawn with a push mower.

—M.R., Texas

〜

I want to write you about a "miracle" that happened in my life 34 years ago today.

My husband and I were bringing home our two girls, 10 and 12, from the Unity Sunday school in W—— where we were living at the time. Just two blocks from our home at a quiet intersection a car from out of nowhere, it seemed, coming at a high speed struck our car with such force that it turned it completely over, pinning me under the car.

My husband and the children escaped with a few bruises. I received a triple skull fracture, a broken cheekbone, a broken nose. The left eyelid was cut so that only half of it would close. The right ear was almost cut off. The left leg was broken, the left knee was crushed, three ribs were broken, three vertebrae dislocated, and there was internal injury. The doctors looked me over and the verdict was, "Not more than four hours to live." Through all the pain, I never lost consciousness. I just prayed.

For two years I was almost blind. My eyes did not focus. When a car or a person came toward me, I saw two of them. For nine weeks I was in a cast from the top of my head to the bottom of my *left foot. I mention all of this to prove that with God nothing is impossible.*

I have been completely healed. I can read without glasses. The skull fractures are healed. The cheekbone and broken nose are normal. My ear healed, and my hearing is fine. The vertebrae are adjusted. I do not limp, and I can walk a mile easily. The internal injury was entirely healed.

The road back to health was long and hard. At times my courage and endurance almost failed. Then one day someone gave me a Unity book. I still have it and love it. Through it, I learned to understand God.

I am now 86 years of age. I thank God every hour of my life for giving me these past 34 years to live usefully. I believe that life is not an impulse working blindly, but a beneficent, rectifying power.

—B.M.H.

It is never too late to learn Truth and know God. Prayer initiates our relationship with God and keeps us connected to Higher Power. With God, nothing is impossible.

You may be wondering if there are any secrets to prayer. Did all of these people experience miracles because they prayed a certain way?

The secret of prayer is that it is simple and straightforward. Let's take a look at some of the fundamentals.

Chapter Three

Prayer That Works

Our prayers are truly empowered when we have a basic understanding of the universal laws at work. The high purpose of prayer is to change our awareness of God so that we express God in all that we think and do. The expression of God is the Truth that is the purpose of life.

What Is Truth?

God is Truth, and thus Truth is Creator of all that is real. There is only one Mind, the Mind of God, and each person is a unique expression of that universal Mind.

Truth is all that is good. "There is no power and no reality in sin," said Charles. "If sin were real and enduring, like goodness and Truth, it could not be forgiven but would hold its victim forever. When we enter into the understanding of the real and the unreal, a great light dawns upon us and we see what Jesus meant when He said, 'The Son of man hath authority on earth to forgive sins.' The Son of man is that in us which discerns the difference between Truth and error."[1] When we understand this, we can free our souls from sin and our bodies from disease.

∽∽∽

Through prayer my daughter had a miraculous healing of cancer, which saved not only her life but the life of her unborn baby.

Last winter my husband J. and I were preparing to go to Cancun for two weeks on a vacation. The day before we were ready to leave, my thirty-year-old daughter M. called and told me that she had gone to the doctor because she thought she had the flu. The doctor told her she didn't have the flu—she was pregnant. We were all excited.

Two weeks later, when J. and I were coming back from the airport, I started to sense that something wasn't right. At home, we found a phone message from M. saying, "Mom call me whenever you get home!" I said to my husband, "Oh my God, it's the baby—something's wrong with the baby!"

As soon as my daughter heard my voice, she began to cry. She told me that the doctor had called her about tests he had done for the pregnancy, and that she had cervical cancer. He had already sent her to a cancer specialist while we were gone. The specialist suggested to M. and her husband that if she tried to carry this baby to term, possibly both she and the baby could die. M. and her husband decided to have an abortion. It was going to be on the next Friday, and she wanted me to come and be with her. I told her yes. We cried and I prayed for her.

Then I immediately called Silent Unity. I also called others to get a prayer chain started. I felt that I was in a paradox. On one hand I was worried about my daughter and grandchild and on the other hand I knew that God was in charge. I was being torn apart at the seams, yet somewhere inside of me I was holding the Truth.

On Monday when I went to call the travel agent to make arrangements to go to my daughter, I couldn't do it. Spirit told me, "Not yet." I follow my guidance, so I decided to wait. On Wednesday M. was going back to the oncologist to get ready for Friday. In prayer that day I got the strong sense that she was to ask for another biopsy. I called her and said, "There have been a lot of people praying for you, and a lot of work in spirit going on. I think it would behoove you to ask the doctor for another biopsy." She agreed.

On Friday, M. called me, crying in relief. "The doctor said there is no cancer! We're going to get to keep the baby!"

Later she said, "I feel like this baby came to save my life, because I didn't even know I was pregnant." I knew that it was true. This was a miracle baby! When I had hung up the phone on Friday, Spirit spoke so clearly to me, "This was also a gift for you. Do you see that it was all an illusion?" I understood then that you can proclaim whatever you want in regards to a diagnosis, but a diagnosis is not the Truth. The Truth is that people have within them an inherent intelligence that knows the Truth. When you get a support system of prayer consciousness going, and the person is open to that vibratory resonance, then absolute healing can take place. It's called "vibratory corollary resonance"—VCR. You have to accept the prayer vibration to heal.

*The doctors then told M. that she would have a premature
birth at seven months. But I told her, "Your mother is going to hold
the high watch. That baby comes here as a gift, and it's not going
to come early."*

*It was an absolutely perfect delivery. At nine months, M.
delivered an eight-pound, six-ounce boy. He's gorgeous, and he's
a good baby. I feel he came to touch many lives on different levels.*

—*T.B.*, Missouri

Jesus talked about the Spirit of Truth as a force that represents God and dwells within. "If you love me, you will keep my commandments," Jesus said. "And I will ask the Father, and he will give you another Advocate, to be with you forever. This is the Spirit of truth, whom the world cannot receive, because it neither sees him nor knows him. You know him, because he abides with you, and he will be in you" (Jn. 14:15-17). When the Spirit of Truth comes—that is, when we awaken—we are guided into "all the truth," he said (Jn. 16:13).

No one can make us see or understand Truth. As Charles observed, "Truth cannot be revealed by one mortal to another."[2] It is an experience unique to each person, a self-discovery made along one's own spiritual journey.

During the course of numerous trials of life-threatening illnesses, one woman's discovery of Truth was that she was meant to witness the healing power of God:

*I've had a lot of miracles. I've had twenty-six surgeries,
including cancers and back operations for ruptured disks, and I
don't know how I still work! In every case, God has healed me
through prayer. I've been involved with Unity since I was very*

young, and whenever I or someone I know needs help, I call Silent Unity. There have been times that I was in a lot of pain or in a hospital alone, far away from my family, and I would break down and cry. But I would always pray, and would listen to the inner voice, which said, "Don't worry."

About ten years ago, I found out that I had polyps in my colon. In particular, there was one that nestled at the junction of the small and large intestines, and the doctor was concerned that it could turn cancerous. At first, I didn't want to do the operation, which meant being cut from above the navel all the way down to the bladder. But in prayer, the inner voice told me I should have it done. So I called Silent Unity.

During the operation, the doctor found that the polyp had turned cancerous. There were two columns of beginning cancer of about four cells each. The doctor cut the small and large intestines apart, removed about six inches from the large intestine and rejoined me. I've had no recurrence of cancer there since.

About four years ago, another cancer developed. I was having hematuria, which is microscopic blood in the urine. It's very common in urinary tract infections. The doctors found a cancerous growth on the bladder and removed it.

About three years later, I became alarmed at an excruciating pain I was experiencing—abdominal spasms. The doctor couldn't explain it, and ordered a CAT scan and an MRI. They found a very large cancer on the head of the pancreas. It measured about 6 x 8 x 10 centimeters. I called Silent Unity immediately and asked for prayers.

The doctor requested that I return the next week for a

bronchoscopic examination, where they stick a tube down your throat and take pictures. My son and husband came with me. While I laid there waiting for the bronchoscopy to begin, I thought to myself, "Well, Lord, if this is it, this is it." I felt calm. I knew that the matter was being taken care of by prayer, especially through Silent Unity. I said, "Lord, it's in your hands."

While I was under anesthesia, the doctor informed my husband and son that I definitely had pancreatic cancer, which was extremely aggressive, and that I probably would die within two weeks to a month. My son, who is thirty-six, cried.

The procedure took an unusually long time. Finally a nurse flew out to my husband and son and said, "There's good news!"

When I woke up, my doctor was standing at the foot of my bed. "I don't understand it," he said. "There is nothing but a big hole where the tumor was." He didn't believe it, so he called in another radiologist. Altogether, five doctors examined the pictures. They all could not believe that the cancer was gone.

Since then, I've had follow-up CAT scans, and nothing has changed. I still have a hole in my pancreas. I have to take a pancreatic enzyme to help digest fat, and I have to watch my diet. But I've had no recurrence of cancer. I know that God removed that cancer permanently, and the Lord never takes away something he has given.

I've been blessed by God in so many ways, but I've wondered why I've had to deal with so many health crises. I think that it is my duty to give witness to God's healing. I wouldn't think of *facing a situation without prayer, because I would feel empty. When I turn to prayer, I feel peaceful. I know that prayers are taking care of me. It's a wonderful feeling.*

—C.M., FLORIDA

We sometimes try too hard to perceive Truth. "Just rest your mind and heart and emotions and body in God-Mind," said Myrtle,[3] and allow illumination to unfold naturally. The Spirit of Truth gives us a right understanding of all we experience and helps us to call upon our powers to meet every need.

Greetings from Wyoming! I want to tell you "Thank You" and to share a remarkable demonstration with you.

I called for prayers for my sister. She had been told her teaching contract would not be renewed—no reason given. Her evaluations were all good.

When I arrived to help her celebrate her birthday, I was surprised and concerned. When she told me her news my mind immediately went to the Daily Word *lesson for the day. It read: "I look beyond every appearance and see the glorious Truth of God." I at once encouraged my sister and told her to try to focus on the affirmation:* This situation does not dismay me, for it is not real. *We went about our celebrations with divine focus, joy, and harmony.*

Upon arrival back in her town on Sunday evening she was told that all the other teachers in her building were sending a letter to the school board, superintendent, and principal. A group of parents were also ready to go to the school board on her behalf.

On Monday I received a call from her. The superintendent, principal, and my sister had talked. Her job was reinstated. Thank You, God! We deeply appreciate all your efforts and blessings. Thank you for assisting her in one more step in her spiritual healing and growth.

—R.H., WYOMING

Myrtle taught the importance of spiritual awakening through study and application of Truth principles, or Christ principles, as she also called them. These principles, applied to all aspects of daily life, are the keys to all good. By turning to God, we connect ourselves to the universal supply.

At Christmas time I replied to your prayer request form. I requested prayer for a financial need, little believing that those prayers would be answered. My lack of faith was surely overcome by the Truth that you saw for me. I am deeply grateful.

Please accept this check for $500, money that I did not have prior to your prayers in my behalf. God does hear those who believe. May He bless you richly, one and all.

—H.D., WASHINGTON

Mental Discipline

The Fillmores said that the best way to find Truth, or God, is by disciplining the mind. We do this by retraining our thinking to eliminate negative, counterproductive thoughts. "By changing your thinking to conform with the Truths of your Being, you will be transformed," Myrtle counseled.[4] The Fillmores stressed repeatedly the ancient and universal Truth that what we think about habitually becomes manifest: thoughts are things. Said Myrtle, "When you keep your mind filled with thoughts of praise and thanksgiving, love and faith, you become a magnet that is irresistible to attract every good and soul-satisfying thing."[5]

I am so filled with gratitude that I must share it with you.

About two years ago I had an eye examination and was told that there was the beginning of a cataract formation. I kept quiet about it and refused to accept it. When I did remember it I banished the thought with some Truth statement such as "God is my instant, constant, efficient help in every need."

I just had an eye examination by the same doctor. This time he pronounced my eyes healthy—no cataract, no glaucoma. I didn't even need new glasses. I am so grateful to God for His ever present help.

I am also grateful to all my Unity friends.

—E.H.D., ILLINOIS

Mental discipline is built up just like physical muscle: regular exercise strengthens it and increases its power. Through mental discipline, we are able to still the mind in order to hear the voice of God. A mind filled with turbulent, angry, fearful, negative thoughts cannot be reached by Divine Mind.

∽⊙∽

It is long past time for me to add my voice to the ongoing "thank you's" that I know come to you.

Do you ever wonder how God resolves the situations you become a part of? I would like to share mine with loving gratitude.

Our telephone rang in the middle of the night. Our son-in-law told us that our daughter was in a birth trauma, and the doctors did not know if they could save either her or the baby.

They live in a rural community, and it would be six long hours before we could fly to them with our love and support. The slang expression "I lost it" best describes what happened to me. It was then that I placed my first phone call to Silent Unity. The warmth of that human voice cut through the icy numbness of my despair. This loving instrument spoke of faith and love and God's caring. But the most valuable message for me was the "job" I had to do. Pacing the floor was not the work of a Truth student. The person instructed me to picture my child glowing with the joy of new motherhood, holding her whole and perfect child in her arms. And so it was. The hours of that night sped by quickly because I was very busy with my work—visual affirmation.

My grandchild has just had her first birthday. She walks holding on, plays blocks with her sister, and giggles when she blows kisses to Grandma.

Those in attendance that night marvel at how much God must need this particular child.
Thank you!

—*D.N.M.,* NEW YORK

〜〜〜

Improving our thoughts automatically affects our words for the better. Our thoughts and words really are one. If we think in alignment with God, then we speak in alignment with God as well. And when we are in alignment with God, we become the expressions of perfect love. As St. Paul observed, we exhibit patience, kindness, generosity, contentment, modesty, goodness and good temper, truth, burden-bearing capacity, faith in everything, a hope for the happy outcome of everything, and never a thought of failure. Perfect love casts away all fear. It is fear that limits us and narrows our vision.

Mental discipline must be followed by positive action—we must live the thoughts and ideals held within the consciousness. We also discipline the mind by focusing our attention in the here and now. Expressing joy and divine love unifies our heart and mind and strengthens our trust with God.

〜〜〜

I am now home after being with my daughter who had brain surgery. She was in a coma for days.
When I telephoned you I was told that all things are possible with prayer. I quit begging and pleading that divine power would heal her. I gave thanks that she was in God's loving care and that all would be well.
My daughter's healing has come about speedily. I feel that

through this ordeal I have gained much spiritually. I have less fear and more trust in divine power.

Thank you for your prayers. May God bless you all and your wonderful work.

—V.C., Canada

Affirmations

Charles defined an affirmation as "a positive and orderly statement of Truth. By affirmation we claim and appropriate that which is ours."[6] For example, an affirmation for health might be: *I enjoy the blessing of perfect health.* An affirmation for finding work might be: *I have the perfect job which is right for me.* Affirmations declare the ideal and desired state of being as though it were already obtained.

Prayer itself is an affirmation. Through it, we set in motion the forces that enable us to manifest the picture of our affirmation. Thus, when we are sick, we do not say we are sick, but affirm that we are healthy. When we are poor, we do not say we are poor, but affirm that we are abundantly rich. To claim our gifts from God, we use denials to remove negative, limiting thought, and we use affirmations to expand our horizons without limit.

It is very hard for me to find adequate words to thank you for your response to my family's plea for prayers.

When I started hemorrhaging internally, the nurses thought I was dying. My daughter phoned you for prayers. I kept thinking,

"I'm not going to die. Silent Unity is praying for me." I came through the ordeal beautifully.

Four months later I was hospitalized for ten days before surgery. The doctors made many tests, and were convinced I had a tumor in my esophagus and also gall stones. The laboratory reports were so confusing. My frightened husband wrote to you for prayers and was so grateful for the personal letter from you.

The surgery showed an ulcer but no cancer anyplace in my body. A week later, as I sat in the X-ray room, I felt a joyous light around me as I affirmed, *"I am a beloved child of God. Every cell of my body is alive with His life, light, and love, and I am now healed."* I knew it for sure, and when the doctor and nurse came back into the room I said, *"I'm healed. Praise God, I'm all healed."*

The X-rays showed no sign of an ulcer, tumor, or anything. The doctor said, *"There was an ulcer here but it's gone. It is completely healed."* The gall bladder operation was so successful I left the hospital in a week. I feel wonderful. I feel great.

How we love Unity and all you stand for. Thank you for your prayers.

—J.H., Iowa

～

My husband had a very severe stroke. I called an ambulance and rushed him to the hospital. At the time, he was completely paralyzed on the entire right side; he could not speak; he had *feeling in only one spot on his left foot; and though he was consicous, he did not know me or know what was going on. I called Silent Unity. I felt I was too upset to be able to do much effective prayer work.*

Shortly thereafter he began to speak one or two words in answer to questions. By the time he was moved to the intensive care unit, he was beginning to try sentences, but could not put more than three or four words together. By this time he recognized me, and was beginning to realize what was happening.

I was then sent to the waiting room and it was six hours later before I was allowed to see him again. All during that time I could think only one phrase—something I had read in a book by Joseph Murphy: "He is the very garment God wears as he moves through this illusion of time and space."

I was by myself and very frightened, but I knew your prayers were sustaining me and resurrecting the healing consciousness in my husband. The nurse came running out to get me saying, "You must come see! You won't believe this! He is sitting up and talking, and moving both arms and legs! It's incredible." We truly had a miracle. The doctors were quite baffled. Thirty-eight hours later he was moved from intensive care to a room and was getting better every minute.

The next morning when I returned to the hospital he said, "Take me home. I can't stand this place any longer." So I brought him home. The doctors and nurses were pretty much upset about this as they thought he should stay at least a week. He is doing better and getting stronger every day. He walks all over the house, and I have to chase him to keep him from doing too much! How can I ever thank you for your wonderful prayers? It is comforting to know you are as close as the nearest phone.

We are both so very grateful and thank God constantly for this miraculous evidence of His presence within. We are praying daily to know that this need never occur again and that perfect health is ours now and always. May God richly bless all of you and the ministry there at Unity Village.

—B.C.E., GEORGIA

∿

Sometime back I wrote to you for help in selling a house and two acres of land. I also wished to sell to a desirable person who would be a good neighbor. A few days past we sold to a real man of God. He and his wife have two children, and they are all we could wish as neighbors.

When my husband would get discouraged, and say, "Well, we are just stuck with the house; no one is going to buy it," over and over I would repeat silently, "All things are possible with God." I never got discouraged. I thank God for your help.

—M.E.T., LOUISIANA

The Fillmores said that mental affirmations are stronger than anything visible in the world. Affirmations drive out the negative thoughts that keep us from achieving our good and from receiving healing. They also help train the mind to right thinking.

⌇⌇⌇

I am happy to report to you of my great improvement and what the Father has done for me. My back is so much better since I learned not to resist the Spirit. When your letter came, I had almost given up all hope, for everyone told me that I would have to have an operation performed and felt that it must be done this week.

After reading your letter, the thought came to me that I was resisting the Spirit, and I said to myself, "Why can't I let go of this fear when the Father has done so much for me?" I then began affirming, "I have faith in the Spirit, and I am free in the freedom of Spirit."

All the pain left me then and there, and I am getting along splendidly.

—Mrs. W.S., OHIO

⌇

I wrote to you for prayers for divine order and protection. I had applied for a position at our local university and had not heard anything.

After writing you, I was called for an interview. And just as I was leaving the house for that big moment, the mail arrived. It contained your letter—the only piece of mail I bothered to open. Inside were several most appropriate affirmations proclaiming that my heart was serene and poised, along with a leaflet that said on the cover, "You Have It!" I cannot describe the assurance your mailing gave to me, as I was on my way to be interviewed by a committee of ten faculty and staff members.

I am pleased to report that the enclosed gift is my first paycheck for being employed in the position for which I interviewed that day. I am nearly overwhelmed by God's love and power, especially when I am told that more than one hundred persons applied for that same position.

In loving gratitude,

—J.B., Minnesota

As declarations of Truth, affirmations should be carefully worded, the Fillmores believed. Words of Truth have real power and take hold in the mind and body to become alive and produce exactly what they say. For example, if we talk about what we have in a negative way, our finances will be decreased, but if we talk about it in an appreciative, large way, we will be prospered, said Charles.

I want to tell you what a wonderful help your prosperity thought has been to me. I needed work, and I looked to the Lord and he heard me. He even gave me more than I asked for. The work simply poured in, and when jobs came that perplexed me, I just asked God to show me, and it was wonderful how the work moved on. When one job was finished, I just repeated, "Thy bounty like a never failing stream, etc.," and before the last garment was finished another or more came from the most unexpected sources. Another thing, I feel so well and strong that people tell me I look ten years younger. I am so grateful for everything.

—*Mrs. A.E.B.,* Minnesota

∼

I want to tell you about my hair. Last April my head was perfectly bare, and everyone had a discouraging word and remedy. I refused all remedies and verbally and mentally said, "God is the life and strength of my hair, and it is coming in just as thick and curly as can be."

Every time anyone would speak of it or I would think of it, I would repeat those words. The result is that my head is now covered thickly with hair about three inches long, and it is just as curly as it can be. Now people say to me, "Isn't it wonderful how your hair grows, and it is so pretty."

—*E.K.,* New York

Myrtle Fillmore believed strongly in the I AM as the most powerful affirmation because it expresses God through an individual's body, mind, and soul. The I AM is the full expression of everything that we are, in the highest spiritual sense. Myrtle recommended use of the many I AM affirmations of Jesus, such as:

"I am with you always."

"Be Still and know that I am God."

"I am the resurrection and the life."

"I am the light of the world."
"I am the health of my people."
"I am and there is naught beside me."
"I am that I am."[7]

Kindly allow me to add my testimonial to the many grand ones published in Unity. When I compare my past life while in the old beliefs (builded upon sand) with my knowledge of today, demonstrating its truth daily, I certainly have reason to be happy and thankful.

Before, there was always sickness in my family, while now health, love and prosperity reign supreme in my happy home. My two dear little boys, seven and eight years old, never have known what sickness is, and I am sure they never will.

My last experience when I threw off the yoke is well worth mentioning. During ten years, I was in pain from a very bad hernia causing me untold suffering. Although strong in my faith as taught through your noble teachings, the beliefs prevailed, and I was brought home a year ago with a strangulated hernia. The best surgeons were called, my case pronounced hopeless, and I was rushed to the [hospital] where the head surgeon after a consultation with his staff told my dear wife that I probably would last three days, when blood poisoning would set in and end my days. My friends, of course, were all duly notified of this fact.

While on the operating table, my ever-faithful wife wired you of my case, requesting your coassistance, to which you nobly responded. The operation was successful, the nurses telling my wife that I boldly proclaimed while under the knife and unconscious, "I am, I am God." On the third day, I even had no fever, and on the fourth my wound was completely healed, to the great surprise of the learned doctors; and now I am a living wonder to them.

Can anyone blame me for resting all my faith in the only Truth?

—J.W.W., Missouri

Blessings also are powerful affirmations. By blessing a problem that needs to be solved, we infuse the situation with divine healing energy.

I was in the process of moving from my residence. The day I started moving, a chemical company came out to service the apartments with insect spray. They saturated everything inside and outside. I've had allergies before, but I was never a person to be sick. Now I found myself severely poisoned. That night, I had great difficulty breathing and was in spasms. I was very frightened. I kept thinking, "This will pass, this will pass." I prayed, and the attack would pass, but then it would come back. This happened repeatedly.

I didn't get better. I tried to heal myself through diet and herbs, but nothing seemed to help. Finally I went to a doctor, who started treating me for asthma. The medications helped me to breathe, but not to heal. I took the drugs for almost two years.

I started asking God, "What do you want me to do?" My lowest point occurred one night before I went to sleep. I said to God, "I know there's a lesson about life in this for me, but I don't know what it is. If it's time for me to go, I'm ready." Then I started blessing everybody I could think of, including anyone who had done or said the least thing to hurt me. I forgave them and blessed them. I forgave and blessed myself. I released myself from the planet. I fully expected to die. I was really surprised the next morning when I woke up.

Over time, God's answer to my prayers was that I should try alternative healing. I started brainstorming. I consulted Myrtle Fillmore's book, Healing Letters. *It became a study for me. I also started working with homeopathic medicines. I decided not to refill my prescription medications. Instead, I concentrated on using Myrtle's method of prayer, and homeopathic medicines.*

I prayed whatever came intuitively to me. I surrendered myself to God. Oh, I focussed intensely on surrender! I prayed, "I release all of this into your care, Father, because I know that your healing is the best." I also used Myrtle's way of speaking to the organs of my body. I let Spirit guide me in what I should think, pray and feel. I claimed my healing and released all that did not serve me.

Within two weeks, I saw a definite improvement. One morning I woke up feeling normal—I was healed. It's taken me some time to regain my strength, but I'm working at it every day through exercise.

One of the lessons that I learned was that prayer really does work. Of course, I knew that it did, but this experience really brought that home to me. Not only does it work for other people it works for me, too.

—*L.M.,* Missouri

∽

If people told the Fillmores that they said affirmations but got no results, Charles told them to examine how they were living. In other words, were their thoughts, words, and actions undermining their affirmations? Affirming something for a few minutes a day does little good if we spend the rest of our time allowing negativity to be expressed. We must walk by the Spirit and put our entire consciousness into the affirmations we are seeking to manifest.

The Importance of Prayer and Meditation

The most important way to discipline the mind, and thus connect with Truth, is to spend regular time in prayer and meditation. Charles and Myrtle Fillmore knew firsthand what a tremendous difference prayer can make in life. If we all applied ourselves to prayer, we could free ourselves of the ills of humanity.

"Prayer is man's steady effort to know God," said Charles. "There is an intimate connecting spirit that logically unites man and his source."[8]

Myrtle referred to prayer as "communion with God . . . . This communion is an attitude of mind and heart. It lifts the individual into a wonderful sense of oneness with God, who is Spirit, the source of every good and perfect thing, and the substance that supplies all the child's needs—whether they are spiritual, social, mental, physical, or financial."[9] Prayers are not "sent" anywhere, she said. "Prayer is an exercise to change our thought habits and our living habits, that we may set up a new and better activity, in accord with the divine law rather than with the suggestions we have received from various sources."[10]

Prayer accomplishes many things. It develops our character to its highest state. It builds a mind that is always open to Spirit. Through prayer, we attain an interpenetrating consciousness with God's perfect life and love and power. We attain a oneness with God, thus achieving the example set by Jesus when he proclaimed, "I and the Father are one." Said Charles, "There is a partial unity with Spirit and there is a complete unity with Spirit. Whenever we wholly merge our mind with creative Mind we meet Christ in our consciousness, and it is when we are in this consciousness that our prayers are fulfilled."[11]

Prayer also changes our very energy field. "Prayer liberates the energies pent up in mind and body," said Charles. "Those who pray much create a spiritual aura that eventually envelops the whole body."[12] This radiant energy is noticeable to others, even unconsciously, and has a beneficial effect.

This radiant energy may manifest quickly, or it may take a while to build up. Prayer releases positive forces that accumulate. In the following letter, we see prayers initiated to resolve problems at work. The call to Silent Unity set forces in motion. Nothing happened immediately, but then an energetic "critical mass" factor occurred after thirty days—the time that Silent Unity spends praying over every request made by telephone or letter.

∼⊙∼

I phoned because I had a problem at work. It was coming to a point that I felt I might have to look for another job. After my phone call, nothing changed for about a month. One Monday morning I went to work, and it was like a miracle.

Everyone in the office seemed to have a new attitude (including me). Now I look forward to going to work. Everyone gets along well and any problems relating to the past have disappeared.

Thank you for your prayers.

—C.P., CALIFORNIA

Sometimes positive shifts in our environment occur quickly.

Whenever you pray with me things work out just the way I would like, but I never write to tell you. I am taking this opportunity to say that everything we have prayed for has been victorious.

Some weeks ago I was having a great deal of unhappiness on my job. We prayed about it. I was pleasantly surprised when my boss called me into his office, apologized, gave me a raise, and asked me to continue working with him.

Please continue to pray with me.

—M.D.K., FLORIDA

And sometimes change occurs more gradually. We aren't aware of it while it is occurring, but we can look back in hindsight and see how much we've improved as a result of prayer.

Eight years ago I wrote to you asking for prayers for my health, my prosperity, and my growing good for the future. I was fifty-eight years old, in ill health, newly divorced, and very, very frightened of the future. To begin the new year, I wrote to ask for continued prayers and again to share the first increase of each raise I got at work. I am now in excellent health. I work full time, my income has tripled, and I have some nicely growing investments as well as a home almost paid for. My three children and six grandchildren tell me I am a joy and a comfort as well as a good, positive friend to them.

I have traveled some, and I hope to do more this next year. I am very busy and happy to be so useful, and I marvel more each year at the good in my life.

May God bless you all for being there in our need, sharing God's eternal good with us. Again, I send my first paycheck increase this year.

—*S.J.B.*, Maryland

Prayer also enables us to become infused with divinely inspired ideas, which exalt our minds and our entire beings. "Every divine idea you meditate upon and incorporate into your consciousness does a mighty regenerating, transforming, spiritualizing work in your mind, soul, body and even in your outer world of affairs," Myrtle said. "Each time you grasp an idea of Truth you lift your consciousness a little higher, and the work of transformation goes on 'until Christ be formed in you.'"[13]

The Power of the Silence

Especially powerful moments are experienced in a meditative state of prayer called "the silence." When we sit in the silence, we become receptacles, or Holy Grails, to be filled with the Divine Mind. In the silence, we are inspired with fresh resolve, with new creative thought, with solutions to problems, and with the understandings of Truth that we need. "We get our most vivid revelations when in a meditative state of mind," Charles said. "This proves that when we make the mind trustful and confident, we put it in harmony with creative Mind; then its force flows to us in accordance with the law of like attracting like."[14]

In summary, we see that:

⚘ We experience our good when we understand and apply Truth.

⚘ We understand Truth when we pray and meditate.

⚘ We apply Truth through mental discipline, affirmations, and right living.

Chapter Four

How to Pray

Prayers are effective when we establish sound prayer habits. As we saw earlier, these include praying daily in an affirmative manner, disciplining our thoughts, applying Truth in our lives, and living our prayers—praying without ceasing, as Paul taught. The Fillmores did not advocate supplicant, begging prayer. All begging does is create mental turbulence that hinders contact with Divine Mind. Rather, prayer should be a means to know God, and through knowing God, we receive the blessings and abundance that are ours.

The Fillmores emphasized the importance of praying with a joy-filled heart. "God is a God of joy," said Charles. "It is through our realization of this truth that we drink heartily of the wine of life."[1] When we pray joyfully, we connect fully with the zest and true purpose of living. We awaken new trains of thought. We unleash powerful healing forces.

Weakened Prayer

Prayer is ineffective when it is accompanied or followed by negative thinking or mindless repeating of affirmations. We have to put power into our thought, change our thought, and believe in the guidance we are receiving. If we spend energy on negative beliefs and feelings, we will get negative results, even if we and others pray daily for us.

"We sometimes think that we pray when we read and declare statements of Truth," said Myrtle. "We have very little idea of the way in which the answers to those prayers are coming. And we do not prove that we expect them to be answered. Almost immediately after praying we go on doing the things we have been doing, which does not allow answers. And we think and say that which is not in accord with the prayers we have made. For example, we go into the silence and declare statements of prosperity. Then in writing a letter we speak of lack and failure and longing which proves that we have those thoughts and feelings of lack in our hearts and that we are dwelling on them more strongly than we are on the Truth that we have prayed."[2] Thus we must *think* and *live* the prayers that we make for them to be effective in getting good results.

Prayer is also ineffective when we pray with selfish motive, such as to manipulate another person to do our bidding. It is rightful to pray for our or another's good—for healing, prosperity, love and happiness—as long as we do not do it with an intent to control another.

Sometimes our selfishness is not deliberate. We get so wrapped up in our problems that we fail to see the forest for the trees.

Attunement to God

We can prevent frustration by properly attuning ourselves to God before we pray. Keep the following principles in mind. Your intent will be clear, and your mind and heart ready to receive God's loving guidance.

SURRENDER TO THE WILL OF GOD

When we surrender to the will of God, we are praying for the highest good for all concerned. This means letting go of a specific desired outcome and being open to the answer that God provides.

⌒⌒⌒⌒

I can't tell you how much it has meant to me to know I could write to you and have help in prayer. I have always had the feeling that you were there when I needed you—like a rock. When my batteries were running low I could hook on to yours and you would recharge me and increase my prayer power and my faith. Your corporate faith never runs dry, but produces miracles.

When I wrote you the other day I felt as though I were disintegrating inside from physical, mental, and emotional exhaustion—too much pressure for too long. I felt unable to function, though I knew that all would ultimately be well, and I wanted only God's will. I was going through a testing time and I was afraid that I wasn't going to be able to hang on long enough, to "overcome evil with good." But as always when you hit bottom, everything worked together at once and blessings came pouring in from every direction, and I saw how everything worked together for good. Spiritual growth doesn't come easy, to me anyway. It required some "healing of the memories." When I ask God to make me whole, He's got to have time and

I've got to have faith. Thank you for everything, especially your faith. May the enclosed love offering be a blessing.

—N.R., Wisconsin

∽

I would like to share an experience with you which changed my life and helped me to turn my life over to God and trust in His power. For the past year, I had been facing a difficult situation in my life which required a final decision to "let go" of an unhealthy relationship. I had been in turmoil for months trying to "let go" of the relationship but only found I was in a deeper struggle because the other person involved chose not to "let go."

Since I had affectionate feelings towards this person, it was painful to see I was causing a lot of suffering for both of us. I prayed to God for guidance, wisdom and strength to help me end this relationship and thought God just wasn't listening or didn't care to help me. What I didn't realize was that I was more concerned about my relationship with this other person than I was about my relationship with God.

On Thursday, April 11, I called Silent Unity. A gentleman answered the phone and asked what I needed to pray about. I explained briefly that I needed God's strength and wisdom to help me in a decision. When the man prayed, I instantly felt God's presence giving me the strength, the courage, and the peace that He was going to take care of everything if only I would trust Him.

Your prayers helped me open up to God to make a decision to trust Him and have peace, or to trust myself and have continuing turmoil. I have ended the relationship with this other person and have found peace in my life by trusting in God's strength and love and the power of praying. I still struggle with the decision from time to time, but I lean on God's strength and love.

I am so grateful for your prayers and for helping me really listen to God. I believe God wants all of us to reach out to Him and to one another in prayer because that is how we feel the power of God's Holy Spirit working in us.

God be with you always.

—V.H., Michigan

∼

Praise God for love and perfect health!

I had written to you for prayers when, after a physical checkup, the doctor found a spot on my lung and said that surgery was necessary. Tests were made and plans for surgery were also made.

I said, "God is in charge." One more x-ray was made, and suddenly it was discovered that the spot was diminishing. In the meantime, you, my husband, and I were praying and knowing that the only presence and power in my body was God the good omnipotent, and that He was in charge. Surgery canceled!

Last night my doctor called to tell me that when another x-ray was taken three days ago the spot was completely disappeared.

He said it was a very unusual and mysterious turn of events. However, I knew that God was in charge the entire time.

This experience has proved to me beyond a doubt that God is always with me, and what a blessing you wonderful dear people of Silent Unity are to me.

I pray now for a more understanding heart and praise God and you for your help in showing me that I can continue to learn and help others as you have helped me.

—M.W.F., CALIFORNIA

PRAY FOR THE HIGHEST GOOD

We often think we know what is in our or somebody else's best interests, when in fact we don't. We might be shortsighted, intent on immediate resolution, or even have misplaced values. Praying for an outcome that is in the highest good of all is open-ended, does not limit possibilities, and ensures harmony.

Some months ago I received news that my son-in law was hit by a car while bicycling home from work. He had been struck on the head and was in a deep coma.

I wanted to pray but I was not sure how to do so. I am not new to the idea of prayer. It's just that since I've become acquainted with the teachings of Unity, I realize the power of the spoken word. I did not want to be selfish in my prayer but to pray for the good of all concerned. I knew I needed help, and it was at that time that I was prompted to call on the help so freely offered by Silent Unity.

The man who answered my call was very kind and reassuring. (I felt as though I had just dialed a direct line to God!) Such a feeling of peace came over me, and I knew then that God would heal my son-in-law. It would just be a matter of time.

What a wonderful feeling of closeness, a oneness that I have never before experienced in that way. I can't explain the joy of knowing that God was at work to start the healing process for my son-in-law's complete recovery. He remained in a coma for seven weeks but is now back to work after only three months.

—B.B., Wisconsin

〜

I hope you will publish this letter, or at least the essence of it. I feel it has a significant message for people like me who tend to lose faith in themselves and wonder if God is still watching over them. Of course, when I am rational, I know that God is with me always; but when I want something desperately and don't have my prayer answered right away, I begin to wonder if I am worthy.

This is the story of answered prayer, but the answer didn't come when expected nor was it the expected answer. I called you in the spring and asked that you pray with me to get a teaching job. I was graduating and wanted very badly to get a job in a certain school district. To my surprise, my prayer was not answered. I had expected an answer within days, or at the most, weeks. Weeks turned to months. I called every month to renew the prayer effort and you were always positive that my prayer would be answered. I wasn't so sure. I went through moments of self-doubt, mild depression, despair. I didn't have faith in myself or in God. I had the valley of the shadow of death—death of self-confidence.

The last time I called, the lovely lady told me, "Now remember, you want the right job." The remark stayed with me. I was able to thank God for the right job, at the right time, and in the right way.

My wait is over, and believe me, I have again learned that God knows better than we do what is best for us. I have a job teaching the very grade level I wanted in a school with all the qualities of love and understanding that will nurture me as a teacher. I will be working with warm, understanding people. I am so thankful. The other school district that I wanted has a lot of problems in many areas. I had wanted to bring God's love to it, but God has given me a place that will give to me. Perhaps I am to learn and grow in the place where love is so available to me so that I can one day go to the ailing school district and help with healing. Perhaps that will not be so. I have always felt that my becoming a teacher is what God wants me to do and that I must do His bidding in my work. I have always felt that wherever He sends me, He has something special for me to do. I look forward to discovering what it will be.

Thank you for always being there and for giving of yourselves so lovingly.

—M.D.G., NEBRASKA

The highest good may not be an easy path to take. When someone we love is sick, we want them healed. Sometimes the healing for the highest good is transition from physical life into life of the Spirit.

I needed help. I called you, and God answered. Frustration can only begin to describe my feelings when I made my call. I had just returned from my birthplace in a foreign country, where my father lay in an intensive care unit at a hospital, being kept alive artificially after a fight with pneumonia. At eighty-four and suffering from severe hardening of the arteries, he had lost brain function some time ago. It was very upsetting to behold the skeleton of a once strong and handsome man being put through so much suffering with no real hope for true survival. I believe in death with dignity, but by the time I made it to him (after being notified of his illness), treatment had already begun. All my efforts to convince doctors to leave him alone, of course, were hopeless. One day he would be almost gone, then they would put him through tortures trying to keep him alive.

I returned home to my family, for there seemed to be nothing left for me to do. **Daily Word** *and* **Unity** *magazines have been my companions now for some time. Suddenly I knew there was something I could do for him, and I called you. Silent Unity started to pray for my father's highest good. He died two days after you* *wrote a beautiful letter. I found your letter when I returned from his funeral. His soul has found beautiful peace, and so have I.*

—C.H., MARYLAND

~

To some this may seem a strange demonstration of God's love, but to me it is one of complete fulfillment.

My husband had been in failing health for several years due to numerous ailments, one of which was a cancerous lung. It had been successfully treated by radiation—and prayers from Silent Unity. We had just returned home after having spent a thoroughly enjoyable Thanksgiving with our two sons and their families when my husband complained of stomach cramps and nausea. Within two days he had lost all strength in his arms and legs. Tests and X-rays revealed an obstruction in the upper intestines, which doctors felt could be treated with medication.

I called Silent Unity that evening, and the lovely lady with whom I talked assured me that my husband was in God's loving care, and that they would also pray for my peace of mind. As always, after calling Silent Unity, I had a wonderful feeling of letting go and letting God do His perfect work.

Later that evening the doctor called to say that my husband's condition was serious, that he seemed disoriented, but was in no pain. They would do more tests the following morning. When I arrived at the hospital the next morning, he was in a coma and was slipping fast, due to failure of his kidneys and liver. That *afternoon I was holding his hand and repeating the twenty-third Psalm, and when I came to the last line:* . . . and I shall dwell in the house of the Lord for ever, *I felt a slight pressure on my hand. With a peaceful sigh, he was gone.*

I cannot express in words my feeling at that moment, other than a feeling of complete "at-one-ment" with God, and a thankful heart that my husband had not suffered, that God had answered his prayer never to have a lingering, painful illness.

I have so much to be thankful for—forty-seven years of happy memories, two wonderful sons and daughters-in-law, and five lovely grandchildren; also many close friends.

When I called Silent Unity to tell them of his passing, their consoling words were so uplifting, and the peace I feel now I know is sustained through your prayers. I also know I shall go on to greater growth, greater understanding, and I am sure, to happiness and joy and fulfillment.

Enclosed is a love offering sent in deepest gratitude to all of you at Silent Unity.

—M.O., CALIFORNIA

PRAY IN FAITH

Charles observed that faith is the foundation of successful prayer and the spiritual life and is our most important power. Faith connects the realm of Spirit with the realm of matter. Hebrews 11:1 tells us that faith "is the assurance of things hoped for, the conviction of things not seen." Through faith, we see the possible and know we can make it real, no matter what circumstances are in front of us. Jesus told us that through faith, even a tiny amount the size of a mustard seed, we can accomplish any-thing—we can do all the great works that he did, and more. "According to your faith let it be done to you," he said (Mt. 9:29). No matter how dire our circumstances, faith enables us to create and transform anew. Charles said that whatever we create in our minds and really put faith in will become substantial.

Our daughter drowned in five inches of water. The doctors confirmed this when we got to the hospital. My faith would not let me believe it. My faith was put to the test that day, for I had to give her completely to God. My prayer was, "She is in Your hands. Let Your will be done." When I spoke these words, I felt more peaceful than I ever had before.

The doctors told us later that they had revived her, but there was very little hope of recovery because her brain had been damaged and her lungs had collapsed. We told the doctor that she would be fine. Before the evening was over, all vital signs were normal, there was no brain damage, and her lungs were working fine. She came home in one week.

When I called Silent Unity, I asked the lady who prayed with me to pray that my daughter would be made whole, and she is!

I know that God hears and answers prayers. If you ask God, and believe, you will get an answer. Thank you for your prayers. May God forever bless you.

—M.R., GEORGIA

It is about time I told you this. You have prayed faithfully with me and for me.

Five years ago I was "hopelessly" caught up on drugs and alcohol. I was extremely withdrawn; it was impossible for me to sleep at night. I couldn't work if I wanted to and I didn't want to. I was painfully sick, mind and soul. I had no trade; my work history was terrible. I had no friends; my parents had given up on me.

Then I started praying the prayer of faith I had learned as a kid. Since then I've had mountainous experiences and have gone through some deep waters, but through those deep waters God has been with me, closer than breathing, comforting me, and teaching me to grow up in every way. No drugs now.

I have a trade and work at it and enjoy it. I sleep at night. I have never known such peace. My wife and I have been tithing regularly for four months now. Unity literature, I read habitually.

A psychiatrist said that a basic characteristic of the mentally ill is self-centeredness, and I know and am ever learning that we must all learn to be God-centered.

Unity is to me a way of life. Thank you.

—B.H., Nevada

To build faith, we must affirm our unity with God and then have faith in the power of that unity. When we place our faith first in God and not in material things and circumstances, then we tap into the power of miracles.

Regardless of what happens in the outer world, we are always guided to perfect our expression of God. When we pray in the faith that there is a flawless pattern for wholeness within every person, we enable that pattern to be expressed. The highest good always manifests when we are open to receiving the answer that is right for us.

⁓⁓⁓⁓

We expected a miracle and we received a miracle! Thank You, Father-God. Thank you, Silent Unity friends. Our "Sleeping Beauty" is awake!

When I heard a little voice whisper over the phone, "I love you Grandmother," I exploded with gratitude. Our twelve-year-old granddaughter had been unconscious for almost three months following an auto accident. The doctors had said she might never regain consciousness, and there might be severe brain damage. But we refused to believe it. Bless them, they just didn't think about the power of united prayer.

I thank God for the lessons we have learned from this experience. I learned to say "Thy will be done" without adding how or when. Sometimes it isn't easy to get our will out of the way and release our loved ones to God's care, but it can and must be done.

I know that with each passing hour God is strengthening J— and soon she will be walking. I thank God for her complete and perfect healing.

My sincere gratitude to all of you in Silent Unity for your prayers, your letters of faith and encouragement, and your phone conversations which helped so much. May the Silent Unity light shine forever!

—M.W., TEXAS

❧

Several months ago I wrote to you asking for prayers for my daughter. She was in danger of losing her job because she was wrongly accused of dishonesty.

At first I was very disappointed when she lost the job in spite of our prayers. I wondered why God would let this injustice happen. But she has since gotten a more stable and rewarding job and is very happy. This made me realize again that our prayers are always answered, but not always in the way we expect.

Thank you for being there.

—S.L., CALIFORNIA

❧

I am pleased to send this offering and my heartfelt thanks to you for the prayers of Silent Unity for me.

I phoned Silent Unity about a month ago requesting them to pray for me in connection with obtaining a position that I thought I wanted very much. The position was not offered to me although I possessed all the necessary qualifications.

Momentarily, I became discouraged, but I knew that Silent Unity was praying and that I must remain steadfast in the realization of God's law of perfect placement, abundance, and love. I did not know what to do next.

Then the thought came to me to send out a form letter to persons in various cities requesting of them information about the type of position in which I was interested. This I did, and I blessed each letter knowing that I had voiced the Truth and that if my having such a position was God's will, something would work out.

I received an answer to one letter stating that there was an opening of the exact type in which I was interested and that a test would be given in just four days. This was exciting news, and I immediately let the matter go personally and placed it in God's hands by saying "Thank you, Father. I know that if this position is my proper place, all will be taken care of. It is up to You. If this doesn't work out, a better position will come to me."

I took the test, knowing all the time that it was not I but God's wisdom flowing through me giving the answers. The very next day I received a long-distance phone call. The person calling said that I had been accepted for the position and asked when I could start to work.

Although I have been a student of Truth for many years, I still find the booklets and cards you sent to be inspirational and a real focus point to still my thoughts and align myself with God and His love.

—H.Y.

RELEASE FEAR

Fear and negative thoughts short-circuit prayer and interfere with receiving our good. If we find ourselves consumed with fear and negativity, it is all the more important to pray. Prayer itself releases fear.

My prayers were answered. How do I begin to thank you for your support during a very difficult time?

When I called you I knew I was going to be out of work soon. I am a single mother raising two teenage daughters and had no idea how I was going to pay my bills and support my girls if I could not find another job. When I first learned I was going to be out of work, I went to God and put it in God's hands. My faith was very strong throughout the process, and I knew God would not let me down. I believe in God's promises. However, as I began to run out of time, I felt myself panicking. I still believed in God's miracles; I just needed some additional support. Silent Unity was there for me.

On December 23 I received a phone call from someone with a job offer, which I accepted. So when everyone asked me if I had received what I wanted for Christmas, it was very easy to say, "Yes, my prayers were answered."

Thank you again for all of your support. It gives me deep pleasure and a true sense of security knowing that all of you are there for me.

—*D.F.,* New York

I called for prayer for our little great-niece. She was premature, weighing slightly over two pounds. Her condition was critical, and she was not expected to live.

*She is now two and a half months old and weighs a big five
pounds! She is allright physically and mentally. She came home
from the hospital to an overjoyed mom and dad and a protective
big brother who is three years old. She is truly a gift of God—our
miracle baby!*

Thank you for your prayers.

—L.K., ILLINOIS

PERSIST IN PRAYER

Many of the letters received by Silent Unity testify to the results of prayer that is continued even when events in the outer world are discouraging. As we have already seen in numerous testimonials, we cannot know how and when the answers to prayer will work out. We cannot give up simply because we may not receive immediate results.

*Thank you for your letter and the beautiful thoughts enclosed.
You wrote that you believed that I would soon have a report to
share with you, and I do.*

*Slightly over a year ago I was dismissed from my teaching job
after five years of successful teaching, and the dismissal was based
entirely upon falsely written statements. I called to you several
times, and always received encouragement. I instituted a court suit
and was successful in getting it on the court docket, even though
the opposition tried many methods to get it dismissed. We are*

fortunate that we have a very fair and fine judge of our circuit court. The school corporation immediately offered me a reinstatement, for they knew they faced an embarrassing situation. I was not given a teaching assignment but placed in a highly pressured job with disgruntled employees and was assigned a job primarily geared for a high school graduate. I took my assignment and gave it all that I had and continued to call you and ask for prayer. One of the bookkeepers tore me to shreds every day and I continued to pray. Amazing things happened. She no longer had those loud outbursts toward me, and she began to help me with my work.

I met one of our new principals from another school. He seemed to be one of the finest men I have ever met. I felt that God had a purpose for me, and I was led to pray for a job with this principal. I used the thoughts presented in one of Mrs. [Catherine] Ponder's books which suggested praying to the angels. I prayed to the angels to open this principal's mind and heart to reveal any good that I might offer for his school. Amazing things happened. I had a letter from the superintendent offering me a part-time job with this principal. I had hoped for a full-time job, and now it appears as if extra duties might be added to make it a full-time job. I know that God is in this situation.

I am enclosing my contribution for your good work. You have helped many people. I am grateful for the prayers that you have offered for me.

—M.M., Indiana

⁓

I wrote to you with a special prayer need. We were having much financial pressure and there was a seemingly insolvable situation involving other people that kept us under this pressure. Strained conditions had existed for more than a year. My husband and I prayed constantly during that year and meditated about the problems we faced. During that time I sought Unity's help often.

We made it through those months of worry and pressure and three weeks ago the situation resolved itself. The people involved, who had made things so difficult for us, who have behaved in a selfish and angry way, made a complete change and became fair and worked with us even more than was ever expected. Truth prevailed and a miracle took place. A final meeting was held, and although we knew in our hearts that God answers prayer and we knew how long we had prayed, we were not prepared for the shock we felt when these people changed their minds and our problems were completely solved in a matter of less than an hour.

We fell to our knees and cried tears of joy when we were alone for we knew what we had just witnessed and experienced. Praise and glory to God. Thank you, Silent Unity, for helping, guiding, consoling, and praying for our situation.

—R.L.B., Tennessee

∼

My wife was diagnosed as having advanced emphysema and was told it would get progressively worse. The doctor prescribed oxygen several times a day.

I called Unity and talked to a dear lady who assured me that my wife was healed. This was difficult for me to comprehend, with all the physical evidence to the contrary, so I took her to the most modern lab in town. They took x-rays and gave her every breathing test available. They found her lungs to be in excellent condition.

That was over a year ago. She was able to stop taking her medicine and soon was completely off oxygen. She has had no further symptoms of emphysema.

We celebrated our 50th wedding anniversary last year, so you know how precious she is to me. Words cannot express my gratitude for your prayers.

Thank you, my dear friends at Unity.

—T.J.P., CALIFORNIA

BE OPEN TO ALL POSSIBILITIES

Answers to prayers come in many ways. God can respond directly, and we hear or understand the words in the mind. Answers can come through dreams. The old saying goes that we should "sleep on it" when we are faced with a vexing problem or a decision. If we pray before retiring, the energies set in motion by prayer can clear the fog during sleep. We may dream about an answer, or a resolution may be crystal clear to us upon awakening.

Answers to prayer can come through the words and actions of other people, through opportunities that open or close, or through things we happen to read. God is constantly feeding us guidance. If we are open to all possibilities, we see that many events of synchronicity, or "meaningful coincidences," are really purposeful messages for us.

~~~

I want to share with you a healing miracle that happened to me.

I had written to you asking for prayers for my back which was broken in a car wreck. One day I was walking on the street downtown. Perhaps I was stooping, giving way to the pain in my back. Anyway, a voice was audible to me saying "J———, straighten up."

I looked around to see who was saying this. I was the only one on the street. Immediately I realized what had happened. I had been healed. I haven't had a pain since. Thank God!

—J.R., Illinois

~

About three weeks ago I wrote you a letter, asking for your prayers. I was faced with a seemingly perplexing situation. I had to get my home financed or lose it. I had had two extensions of time; the last would end September 1. This worrisome condition loomed before me, and I was much disturbed. My application for financing had been turned down by four building and loan associations because of the failure of a business, a partnership, that I was once in.

A man whom I have known only a short time, and with whom I have had only one business transaction, came to my rescue. He agreed to take over the financing on terms that I can afford. His coming to my aid was an act of God.

Your prayers were the greatest help I have received in many years. I shall send an offering within the next few days. I could not wait to thank you.

—J.R.C.

Our intuition can prompt us to take action that may seem mysterious to us at the time but which reveals the answer to a prayer.

I called you to put my son on your prayer list. He was depressed and had been out of work for three months. During the past weekend, he had another upset. He attempted suicide and has hardly stopped crying for a week. When he left for job interviews this morning he was still crying. I immediately called Silent Unity again and explained the situation.

You prayed with me and told me there was a job waiting for him—a job he would be perfectly happy in. You said the door was open for him and he would walk through it.

He returned home at 1 p.m. I was concerned because I knew he had an interview at 1 p.m. and another at 3 p.m. He said he was driving down the road about four miles from our house when something told him to turn on the road to the right. He followed the road to a dead end. He turned around to come back and saw a big building with a large open door on the right side (he had not

*seen it when he had gone down the road a few minutes earlier).
He obeyed an inner voice to go inside. The manager was busy
talking to a salesman. My son waited for nearly an hour for him to
finish. He told the manager he'd come for a job. The manager took
his name and phone number and asked him into his office. He
didn't even have him fill out an application nor did he ask for
references. He said, "Be at work tomorrow morning at 7:30." Then
he looked at my son and said, "I don't know why I'm hiring you. I
don't need another man."*

*The job is for metal fabrication welding—just what my son's
degree is in.*

*As he was leaving, the manager said to him, "If something
makes you unhappy here, please tell me and we'll do something
about it because I don't want to lose you."*

*Isn't this beautiful? Isn't God beautiful? Isn't Silent Unity
beautiful?*

—*D.W.*, SOUTH CAROLINA

GIVE THANKS

Every time you pray, remember to be thankful. Give thanks for all that you are blessed with in life. Give thanks for the answers to your prayers, even before you know them. Acknowledge that the answers are in concert with divine order, working out for the highest good of all concerned.

Thank you so much for your continuous prayers for my aunt who was diagnosed as having failing kidneys. This condition was complicated by diabetes. The doctor said she wouldn't live through the weekend. The family was called to pray for her. I called for the prayer help of Silent Unity.

I am happy to say my aunt lived through the weekend and has been released from the hospital. The doctor said, "It was more than a miracle." She has now regained the use of her kidneys. Thank God!

—*R.S.*, CALIFORNIA

~

Many thanks once again to Unity. My call for help has been answered in a most remarkable way. All the best we had asked for has happened.

I called to ask for prayers for my sister-in-law and her unborn child. The doctors told us there was very little hope that either one would live. Surgery the next day went well. A boy was born with perfect health. There were a couple of problems with the mother but time has helped these, too.

It was such a beautiful moment. The nurse let us see and touch the baby about ten minutes after his birth. We could do only one thing—give thanks and praise to God. Thank you again.

—*S.M.*, WISCONSIN

The more we turn ourselves toward God, the greater healing and prosperity we experience. Our prayers are answered in ways we cannot anticipate or imagine. We experience tremendous growth of the soul, which in turn nourishes the physical life.

How to Pray

In summary, here are some guidelines for the development of good prayer habits:

- ❀ Pray to understand and embody Truth.
- ❀ Pray to manifest the will of God.
- ❀ Pray for the highest good for all concerned.
- ❀ Pray in an affirmative manner.
- ❀ Pray joyfully.
- ❀ Follow prayer with appropriate changes in thought and action.
- ❀ Be persistent.
- ❀ Have unshakeable faith.
- ❀ Release fear and negative thoughts.
- ❀ Be open-minded about how prayer will be answered.
- ❀ Use the power of united prayer through Silent Unity and other prayer groups and chains.
- ❀ Always give thanks, both before and after the answer is received.

The following chapters illustrate the many ways that the power of prayer works wonders—for prosperity, for healing, for relationships, for addictions, for finding what belongs to us, and even for the welfare of animals and the protection from the adversities of the elements. Each story is true, taken from the pages of the book of life. Many of us initially turn to prayer as a last resort, because nothing else has worked. In so doing, we discover that the answers, help, and spiritual uplift were waiting for us all along. The results of making the deep connection to the Source of All Being is described in this testimonial:

Your prayers work so beautifully and inspire me so much I cannot find words to thank you. I feel in a very tangible way the warmth of your prayers.

With your prayers in the last few months, you have no idea how smoothly everything has worked.

My thoughts and prayers join with yours in sincere gratitude, in love and faith, as you send your love and prayers out to all whom you so magnificently help.

—*G.B.,* NEW YORK

In our challenges and trials, prayer helps us to restore balance and to find God. Once we discover the power of prayer, it becomes the guiding beacon in all matters—truly the light that shines for all.

Chapter Five

All Prayers Are Answered

It is a fundamental of Truth that all prayers are answered.

Prayer answers all needs. No matter what faces us in life, we can pray about it and receive an answer. In the century-plus that Silent Unity has been providing prayer service, thousands upon thousands of testimonials have been collected attesting to miraculous and often immediate answers to both the direst and simplest of needs.

———

I know prayer works, as my husband called Silent Unity while I was in intensive care unit for approximately seven days at [hospital], Missouri, for traumatic brain injury.

The family was told by doctors that the next 72 hours would be critical because I had a closed head injury with (C collar) frontal contusions and small subdural hematoma. I had trauma from a ten-foot fall from a ladder on to a concrete floor, with laceration to the back of the head. My sister told me that the doctors weren't sure if I would make it or not.

This accident occurred on the day before Christmas. What a way to celebrate Christmas. I asked God to give me some guardian angels to get me through this, and my guardian angels were everyone that prayed for my recovery, and the paramedics, physicians, nurses, hospital staff, etc.

Thanks again to the workers at Silent Unity that prayed for me when I was in so much pain because of my head injury, back and neck injuries.

God gave me a gift of life for my Christmas present. Even the physicians noted my miraculous recovery as I improved each day and was released from rehabilitation unit to outpatient therapy three times a week late January.

While I was unconscious and in tremendous pain, I called out to God, and my prayer was answered.

—K.H.B., Missouri

∼

Thank you for your prayers for my daughter. I have waited to send my love offering until now so I could tell you the glorious truth of answered prayer.

My daughter suffered cardiac arrest and was rushed by ambulance to the hospital. She was in intensive care only two days, in a private room three days, and went home on the sixth day. She has been advised by her doctor to rest at home only three weeks before returning to work. All of this shouts of a miraculous healing! Ten years ago she had open-heart surgery,

*which made her quick recovery even more miraculous to doctors
and all the hospital staff.*

Thank you again for continued prayer. Blessings to all.

—*E.M.,* NEVADA

Yet, while we may marvel at such miracles, each and every one of us has had situations in which we have prayed for help, sometimes desperately, and the answers we have sought were not forthcoming. Instead, we have faced pain and suffering, or someone we love has faced pain and suffering.

Jesus told us, "Ask, and it will be given you; search, and you will find; knock, and the door will be opened for you" (Mt. 7:7; Lk. 11:9). If we ask, why do we not always receive? Understandably, we then wonder if some prayers are answered and others are not. Why is one person helped through prayer and not another? Does the way we pray make a difference? Is God simply selective in answering prayers?

The apostle James said that when we don't seem to get an answer to prayer we "ask wrongly" (Jas. 4:3). That is, we are not in attunement with God. Prayer itself is an attunement to God. In asking, we are seeking to tap into the Divine Mind for help and guidance. God holds perfection of all things. This is what we seek—the ability to make perfect our imperfect world. We ask rightly, then, when we pray from the sure knowledge of and belief in God's allness and perfection. As many Silent Unity testimonies show, our surrender and attunement to Divine Mind enable miracles of healing to flow forth into the world, sometimes in an instant.

In fact, all prayers are answered and are answered immediately. Psalm 139:4 tells us, "Even before a word is on my tongue, O Lord, you know it completely." God hears our prayer in the moment we conceive it. And in that same moment, the answer is given.

＊

Thank you for your prayers and help for my son in getting employment.

It seems that when I write you, and the letter is on its way, the prayer is already answered.

Thank you all. I thank God for all His blessings and all of you as His messengers.

My son received his position and is happy with it; he also gives thanks.

—M.E., MICHIGAN

Remember what Charles said about answers to prayer that come quickly: "Speedy answers to prayer have always been experienced and always will be when the right relations are established between the mind of the one who prays and the spiritual realm, which is like an electrical field."[1] If we make it our first priority to have the right relations with God, we have the right "electrical field" of consciousness for receiving the answers to prayer.

How Prayer Is Answered

There are three fundamental answers to all prayers: "yes," "not yet," and "another way." God never gives us a "no" and leaves us hanging. Even when what we pray for is not forthcoming, answers to prayer guide us to look in another direction. God always gives us the opportunity to manifest our highest potential, whether it be through accomplishment, love, forgiveness, or even sacrifice.

THE ANSWER OF "NOT YET"

Why do we receive "not yet" as an answer? Surely we are ready for a course of action, or we would not pray for it! There are various reasons:

❀ Barriers to attunement may need to be broken down so that the transforming, healing power of God can flow through us.

∼∞∼

When I called you for help with my healing need, you sent me a letter saying that you were looking forward to my sharing "a report of blessings received." This, then is a report of my blessings.

The marvels I have to report are far greater than anyone could have reasonably expected. But isn't that what makes for a miracle?

I had been diagnosed, after a long period of time (two years), as having epilepsy, severe and incurable. It seemed to all outward appearances that the seizures which plagued me day and night would not yield to medicine. I did not know what malady would strike my brain and nervous system at random times, leaving me completely helpless, unable to think clearly, to speak, or even to move at all.

I have been a Unity student for several years. My desire for life and healing was intense. I began to study Unity on my own when I was no longer able to go to the local church. I found solace in the healing cassettes you offer, as reading was impossible for me much of the time. People at Unity prayed with me. I tried to use the principles I was learning to unlock the prison of my illness. Gradually, I began to feel that I would be completely healed.

Only one week before my complete and total healing, I lay in a hospital emergency room, severely incapacitated because of hours of successive seizures. At that time I had a spiritual experience. I felt that God was saying in the moment of my most profound suffering that I was healed, that the paralysis was only an outward appearance. That I was well.

In less than one week, I was totally free of seizures. I celebrated my birthday—my re-birthday—exactly one month after Silent Unity began praying for me! I am now completely off the huge doses of epilepsy medication. I have taken up my life again, and I feel so joyful, grateful, and alive that I wished to share it with you. I can hardly stop smiling for a moment! It is so very beautiful to think that I could have a miracle, too.

Many thanks, dear unseen friends.

—J.W., Virginia

❀ There is other work that we need to do in order to bring about the desired results. We've put the cart before the horse, and the answer directs us to re-examine the situation.

❀ We must take others into account. When we pray for others, their own attunement, beliefs, thoughts, fears, desires, and perceived limitations enter into the picture as well. We can send them the healing radiance of prayer, but it is up to them to receive and absorb it.

It's high time I wrote a good report for my husband's sister for whom we asked prayers about a year ago.

She had been fighting cancer for 12 years, and upon its last reappearance the doctors told her that they could not operate again, neither could she stand anymore radium or x-ray treatments. They gave her some hormones and vitamin pills, but held out no real hope for her recovery. She had to give up teaching. She became extremely thin and suffered greatly from large quantities of fluid forming in her abdomen.

When we wrote for prayers, she began to gain in some ways immediately, but her healing was delayed. Meanwhile, through various channels, certain books and truths she evidently needed in order to make the necessary mental, emotional and spiritual adjustment came to her. Almost everyone she knew was praying for her—Silent Unity, Protestants, Catholics, Jews, and those who claim no church affiliation.

Late in May, she had to be tapped, and seven quarts of fluid were removed; but the fluid began to form again immediately, and in a month it was as bad as before. Then all of a sudden, without further medical help, it began to disappear, and in another month she was well. In the middle of July, an astounded doctor told her she could renew her contract and go back to teaching in September. In August she drove her car 100 miles out here to visit us. She was of normal weight and a picture of radiant health.

*She is enjoying teaching her 39 first graders. She seems
literally to have been recreated.*

—L.L.

Charles said that "one who prays for the health of another should understand that it is not the fault of the healing principle that his patient is not instantly restored. The fault may be in his own lack of persistency or understanding; or it may be due to the patient's dogged clinging to discordant thoughts. In any case the one who prays must persist in this prayer until the walls of resistance are broken down and the healing currents are tuned in."[2]

This is why prayers for entire races or countries, such as for the end of strife or warfare, require persistent, large-scale effort. When enough people—the critical mass factor—are willing to receive the prayer energy, the answers can manifest.

THE ANSWER OF "ANOTHER WAY"

Sometimes we are given the answer "another way." When we pray, we usually have a fixed idea of what we want to happen. Only the Creator can know what is in our highest good.

"Another way" is a gentle reminder to us to focus our prayers on outcomes in the highest good for all.

*I called to request prayer for my sister-in-law. She had a brain
hemorrhage and was in the intensive care unit at the hospital. The
prayer was comforting, and she awoke for three days to talk to
everyone and to see all her children.*

*We are all very thankful for that time, as she passed on
New Year's Eve. All of the family, especially her husband, will
be eternally grateful for the time allowed them to converse those
last days of her life, when the doctors had given up on her the
first day.*

Prayer was answered.

—M.B., Oʜɪᴏ

If we earnestly seek guidance through prayer, we must be open to divine direction and we must be prepared to accept and follow it. God always gives us the answer that is right for each situation.

Sometimes what is in our highest good is something we have not expected. Charles pointed out that the soul must grow as well as the body. "So if you find yourself disappointed because you do not at once demonstrate health or success, be at peace and know that your earnest prayers and meditations are working out in you a soul growth that will yet become manifest beyond your greatest hopes," he said.[3]

In being shown alternative solutions and courses of action, we are being guided to surrender and to improve our love, faith, trust, and other God qualities.

We also must do more than merely ask. Remember that Jesus also told us "search, and you will find; knock, and the door will be opened for you." In other words, do everything you can to bring your prayer into manifestation! God does not work alone but asks us to be co-creators in establishing his beauty, wholeness, and harmony.

Is there anything that we can't or shouldn't pray for? Prayer is the holy instrument of the outworking of God's will in the world. If we pray for healing, improvement, enlightenment, love, forgiveness, harmony, beauty, peace, and Truth—in short,

Godly qualities and principles—we will always be in concert with divine will. We should never use prayer in an attempt to manipulate others or to bring harm to others.

Ever since its beginnings, Silent Unity has received more prayer requests for healing than any other matter. After healing comes prosperity—financial, job, school, and professional success. People also seek prayer for their pets and livestock, for safety when traveling, for protection from bad weather, and for the return of items that have been lost or stolen. Sometimes callers or letter writers confess that they feel "silly" making a prayer request. Silent Unity assures them that no request is too small for God's attention.

Chapter Six

Healing Body, Mind, and Soul

The experience of Silent Unity shows that when we turn to prayer, it is usually for healing. Faith-filled prayer brings tremendous healing power, asserted Charles Fillmore. "Healing currents of life are freed and flow into and through soul and body, healing, redeeming, uplifting the whole man."[1] Charles also said that of all prayer requests, those for healing—when made in faith—are the most speedily answered. "The reason for this is that the natural laws that create and sustain the body are really divine laws, and when man silently asks for the intervention of God in restoring health, he is calling into action the natural forces of his being."[2]

Myrtle observed that the Christ pattern for us is perfection. This is the spiritual body referred to by Paul—the perfect counterpart to our physical body. "There is no such thing as a 'disease' or incurable condition," she stated. "These activities, weaknesses, or abnormalities to which the medical profession gives name are but the efforts of the God-given inner intelligence to deal with conditions that the individual has produced by his failure to understand the Truth and to recognize himself as the perfect child of God, and to live by the divine law of life."[3] In healing, we must begin by rejoicing in the perfection of our pattern as a gift from God. We accept our perfection and bring our mental attitudes into alignment with the divine law of health.

Perhaps I am doing the wrong thing in looking back, but I feel I must write you at the risk of repeating myself.

I called you for your help one night—and again you gave me loving help—after two fine doctors told my son and my two daughters that I could never walk again because of a slipped disk in my spine and arthritis in my entire body. They said that they had done all they could, and that the intense pain I was suffering would continue always.

My healing has been slow but sure. I can walk and have walked beautifully, and although pain has been slow in leaving, it is leaving!

Today, the day after this came to me a year ago, I feel such a deep sense of gratitude that I felt I must write you. I said when I entered the hospital that I would walk and be healed, and as I took my walk this morning tears of happiness filled my eyes. I kept repeating, "Thank You, God, and thank you, my Unity friends" over and over. I kept saying this as I walked upright with a fine step and no pain at all!

Again, thank you for your loving care by prayer. And I pray that everyone everywhere will turn to God and experience His beautiful love that I know is mine.

God bless you.

—G.M.H.

Sickness does not exist in Truth. By realizing a healing prayer, we illumine our consciousness with Truth, and it begins to work out our health problems for us, Charles contended. When we begin to work in concert with the Divine Mind, a great new power is added to our consciousness.

∼

We write this letter on the eve of our son's next MRI. Our son is now almost five years old. He was only 13 months old when diagnosed with a malignant brain tumor. The doctors told us we would lose him within two years. They said that no infants ever survive pineal blastoma brain tumors.

We started right there and then asking Unity to pray with us. Your prayer line has given us the strength and courage to go through chemotherapy, a bone marrow transplant, and the emotional turmoil that goes along with a life-threatening disease.

Today, the doctors called our son a "miracle" and that he is! You can see the light of God in his eyes and the joy of life in everything he says and does. Tonight, as usual, I'm getting ready to call Silent Unity to pray for God's will in the healing process.

We thank you for years of love and support.

P.S. I'm writing this in the morning after the MRI. All was clear and there is no sign of the tumor having returned. Once again, we thank you for your prayers, and we hope you realize how much we appreciate all that Silent Unity has done for our son and family.

—S.W., NORTH CAROLINA

Prayer brings us into alignment with the Mind of God so that healing energy can flow through us, either for ourselves or for others. It is not unusual to experience that connection and flow—perhaps as a warm, loving presence or light, or a "feeling" in the body of being healed.

Two years ago I had my right breast removed due to cancer, and while in the hospital they found something on my liver, and the biopsy showed no cancer cells there.

I had to have the MRI test, and while in the tube (where you are not supposed to move), the thing malfunctioned. They pulled me out to call the manufacturer for instructions. My sister who was in the waiting room went to the telephone and called you.

When they rolled me back in the MRI, I kept my eyes closed, but I felt this warm, loving glow surround me, and it held me so snug and comfortable. When they pulled me out, the nurse explained I had been in there two hours and it was great that I did not move because they were able to complete all the tests.

It only seemed like a second I was in there. When I told my sister this, that's when she told me she had called Silent Unity and the kind lady had prayed for God's healing light and love to surround me, and that is just what happened in the MRI chamber.

It has been two years since I had cancer with none showing up anywhere else. When they tested the lymph nodes, hormones, etc. I did not have to take chemo, radiation, or medications. Praise

God for your prayers and the healing light and love He surrounds me with.

    Lovingly yours,

                                          —M.L., Texas

〜

I am very happy to write you of my wonderful healing. My hip was broken and seemingly would not heal. There was nonunion of the fragments of bone, and the doctors said that only a miracle could cure me. I wrote to you and I prayed day and night that through our prayers God might heal the fracture. Several days later I was lying quietly in my bed when I felt as if something moved in my hip, and it hurt for some hours. I suddenly realized that I was healed. It is several weeks since the doctors removed the cast, and the miracle has happened. A strong fibrous growth had formed across the fracture, and I shall be able to walk again. I thank you with all my heart for showing me how to appreciate the great power of God in my life.

                                      —A.C., California

The Fillmores were often asked how long it would take for healing to happen. As we saw earlier, time does not exist in the realm of Spirit. Thus all prayers are answered immediately. If we understand this and understand Truth, healing happens immediately as well. If we have not realized Truth, then time does enter into the picture. Explained Myrtle:

The time element does not enter into spiritual healing. There is no time in Spirit, and all answer to prayer is instantaneous. "Before they call, I will answer; and while they are [yet] speaking, I will hear" [Is. 65:24 ASV]. The work of the Spirit has really begun in you even before you have sent your letter. However, time enters into man's mortal concept of things; therefore the time required to bring about healing in the outer depends upon one's ability to realize Truth and to bring it into manifestation, through his faith and his spoken word.⁴

The Fillmores also stressed that there is much more to healing than recovery from illness or accident. True healing occurs when we advance ourselves spiritually. We awaken to the Christ consciousness within. This soul-awakening unifies body, mind, and spirit.

ᴗᴗᴗᴗᴗ

After 15 weeks, I am able to write and thank you for your prayers. My sister wrote to you for prayers when I was almost killed in an automobile accident.

Fourteen of my ribs were fractured, and my neck was broken. I was in a hospital for six weeks, flat on my back with a traction splint holding my head and neck. The ribs were not even taped, but they healed, and today I am up and around and getting stronger each day.

The doctors were amazed at my recovery and said they wished more patients studied Unity literature.

I have been a student of Truth for 25 years, and many years ago I visited Unity headquarters in Kansas City. My friends at our local Unity center sent loving prayers when I was injured, and I feel certain that your prayers, the prayers of all my friends, and my knowing the Christ within have helped me to recovery. Thank you all.

—G.M.

∼

Last January, when I went to the hospital for a third cancer operation in five years, I just could not find the positive attitude that had sustained me through two earlier operations. The other times I had been able to turn all my worries over to God with astonishing results.

The last time I was very negative and just could not accept God's help. Even so, I went through the operation very well and was almost ready to go home when complications set in. Four days later the doctors were still unable to help me. Both our daughters had left their families to be with us. My husband was recovering from pneumonia. That Thursday is etched into my memory. I was so ill, and everything looked grim. My daughter was sitting beside me, and she was able to say just the right things to help me relax. A while later, she asked if I'd been asleep. I hadn't, but I had been able to go deep inside and find the Christ Spirit where I learned what had to be done for my recovery. On Saturday I was able to go home.

The reason I am writing this is to tell you where my help really *came from. I learned later that my friend had called Silent Unity, and she and another friend had spent that Thursday afternoon meditating on my recovery. I know that this chain of events—Silent Unity, my friends, and my daughter's words were the real reason that I could accept God's help. I have come to believe that the word* accept *is the most important word in our vocabulary. GOD is always ready to help us, but we must accept His help.*

My thanks are long overdue but were sent to Silent Unity from my heart long ago. I learned from this experience, and I believe those close to me did too, how a negative attitude can harm us while a positive one opens the way to all the help we will ever need.

—*L.R.,* Nebraska

∼

I called you requesting prayers for my husband, who was suffering from a severe attack of multiple sclerosis. He has had multiple sclerosis for about twelve years but had never had an attack of this type before. His neurologist did not hold out much hope for anything more than a slight recovery.

Within twenty-four hours after my call to you, he began to regain lost mobility. Now, four weeks later, his condition is almost as it was before the onset of the attack; and he is still improving.

My husband's physical progress is enough for gratitude, but we have more to thank you for.

We now read Daily Word *each morning and share in its lessons and prayers. We are growing in unexpected ways—attitudes, values, goals, and habits are undergoing changes. We now experience joy in small things and are appreciative of our blessings—the world unfolds.*

We thank you for revealing fulfillment in spiritual health, as well as your prayers for my husband's healing.

—*S.L.,* Washington

Charles said that the secret of healing miracles, and of all miracles, is that the mind rules matter. The miracles of Jesus were performed according to universal laws that we can learn to use ourselves. Spiritual ideas move the mind, and the mind moves the body. Jesus merged his mind with the Mind of the Father. His works, he said, were done through the Father abiding within him.

All thoughts radiate energy and set forces in motion. When thoughts are strong enough and radiated over time, they become real. When we lift our thoughts to merge with the Mind of God, our thoughts radiate with the speed of spiritual light and bring to pass healing, health, and wholeness.

Thus, when we are awakened, we understand how our thoughts affect our well-being. "We shall find the body responding instantly to our every thought," said Myrtle. "As we sustain ourselves in peaceful, poised thinking, the body will be renewed in strength and become radiantly healthy."[5]

I can't begin to tell you how much Unity has changed my outlook on life. The power of prayer is thunderous!

For the past six years I have been sorely troubled with arthritis, even to using a cane.

Through prayer and thankfulness the disease has left my body. I walk freely, joyously, and thankfully. God bless you all.

—A.P., Cᴀʟɪғᴏʀɴɪᴀ

～

I received your letter in response to mine, for which I deeply thank you. Some time ago I telephoned your Prayer Room. I had been in an automobile accident. Although the financial matters had been taken care of due to prayer, I was still in pain. It was so bad, I couldn't lie down or sit or sleep.

I called at 9:00 a.m., and within an hour or two my pain was relieved. I had been suffering from two cracked ribs, but although the doctor said it would take six weeks for them to heal I am so improved I feel healed already! I have slept well since my phone call to you. I can do my housework and I can type. I am still stiff and sore, but I have complete faith that God's work is being done. This past week miracle has followed miracle. I have felt that a veil was drawn away from my eyes. I have felt a new understanding of other people, and I have released all animosity from my own heart. It has made all the difference in the world to me. I feel I am truly trying to express God.

—L.F., Mɪᴄʜɪɢᴀɴ

One particular type of healing miracle is reported again and again to Silent Unity: the mysterious disappearance of a tumor, especially cancerous. The tumor vanishes just prior to surgery, or doctors operate and find no tumor. Similar circumstances have been reported concerning gallstones and bleeding ulcers.

Two weeks ago I called right before my Dad was to go into surgery to remove what they believed (98 percent chance) to be a malignant tumor. When we prayed, I was told that healing had begun, and so it had.

I am happy to report that there was no tumor, only infection, which is being treated with antibiotics.

Thank you so much for your support. We praise the work you do as well as the good Lord above.

—L.F., CALIFORNIA

I want to first give all the glory and praise to God, the divine one.

I called you last month for prayer about a growth in my right breast. I had to go back to the doctors on February 22nd for them to look at it again.

On the 22nd, Thursday, I was able to praise God at the hospital because the doctor couldn't find any sign as to where the growth was. They had drawn a picture of my breast; they also had taken pictures of it. But thanks be to God and your prayers, it's gone.

Hallelujah, it's gone. *I just wanted to send you this praise report. Thank you all and may God continue to bless and keep you in the praying business.*

—*T.B.*, Pennsylvania

～

It was with relief that I talked with a very kind person when I called you for prayer. The man was patient and reassuring. I had been having what appeared to be intense gallbladder pains for several hours each night. While we talked of plans to have prayer together, the pain began to lessen.

Several trips to the clinic for tests and examinations determined that I needed gallbladder surgery and surgery for a liver blockage in which there was an apparent cancer. To be more certain, the doctor decided to send me to the hospital.

After several tests, my doctor greeted me with, "No one could have come out of all this with such a good report!" To this I answered, "It is only God who does miracles." The doctor told me that I'd had two miracles. First, they did not find a single gallstone! Second, there was no cancer causing the blockage as the doctor had suspected.

Needless to say, both the doctor and I were elated and thankful to God for this great happening. My nightly pains stopped, and I feel good again.

I wish to thank my prayer partner for his kindness, patience,

*and compassion. His leadership was such help and encour-
agement!*

—E.K., Illinois

———⟨⟩———

Even tumors declared to be inoperable have disappeared after prayer.

———⟨⟩———

*Over the past couple of years I have called for prayer several
times and thought you might like to know what happened.*

*Two years ago I was diagnosed with cancer. I had a large
inoperable tumor in the upper part of my stomach and was treated
with chemotherapy and radiation over a period of 11 months. It
remained stable for a time after that, but when I went in for a
scan this year, I was told it was recurring and showed an increase
in size of about 20 percent. I called my church, my friends, and
Silent Unity.*

*Two to three weeks after having been told this, I had a bone
marrow test, and in a few days I checked into the hospital for a
needle biopsy. I was administered a tranquilizer and then put
into the scanner to pinpoint the area on which the needle biopsy
would need to be done. Finally a nurse came in and said, "Good
news!"*

*The doctor and another nurse came in; the doctor asked if I had
been taking medication, and I told him, no. After comparing this
scan with previous scans, he could find no trace of the tumor—
only a scar where it had been. Everyone was amazed, including*

*myself. They told me I could go home. I can't describe my
feelings—what mixed emotions I had. I've heard of miracles, but
I guess I didn't expect to be a part of one. I don't know why it
happened, but I thank God for every beautiful day I have.*

*I want to thank all of you for the prayers and support. The
people who answer the telephones are knowledgeable and
understanding. I'm so thankful to have them to talk with in
difficult times.*

—D.A., CALIFORNIA

～

*I called and asked for prayers for my son, who had a brain
tumor. The doctors said he could not be operated on as the tumor
was so deep in the brain. They diagnosed his condition as
incurable and said that he would not live.*

*His left eye was closed and the right side was practically
paralyzed. He could not walk alone. His speech was inaudible. I
had to print the alphabet and point out the letters to understand
what he wanted. I always had to feed him.*

*I know that God heard our prayers, because a miracle did
happen. The doctors now say that the tumor is gone; his left eye
has opened and he can walk alone. His speech is as good as ever,
without speech therapy. He is now back in school and can write
with either hand. I am asking you to keep praying for him. And I
am thanking you for your prayers, past and present. Only God
knows how I believe in prayer.*

I am sending a donation and I pray that God will bless it and I hope it will help get God's message across to someone else who needs it. Thank you again.

—E.B., Colorado

When medical conditions are grave, patients often hear the words "no hope" from their doctors. Doctors do their best to assess a situation and feel that it is vital to be honest with their patients. We invest doctors with great authority, and when they tell us something, we are inclined to take it as the final word. However, telling patients that they have no hope may prematurely close the door on their faith in miracles. How many patients give up on recovery because their doctors tell them it would be impossible?

There is *never* no hope! We should never give up seeking divine help through prayer.

Remember that healing and recovery are not always the answers for the "highest good" in every situation. However, testimonials sent to Silent Unity tell of remarkable "no hope" cases that responded to prayer.

May I share with you a wonderful true story of a healing?

A little woman of about 70 years of age, a neighbor, came to me recently and said that her daughter in a distant city had cancer of the intestines. Naturally, she was very much upset, and she could neither eat nor sleep. She wanted to go to her daughter immediately. Her family did not think she should try to go because in her distraught condition she would upset the daughter. I asked her if she would like me to place the daughter's name with the prayer ministry and in the noonday silence prayer box at the Unity center where I am a worker. She said, "Please do. Their prayers have helped me, and I know they can help M—." So the daughter's name was entered in both places.

Arriving home this evening, I found the neighbor much more calm and serene. She told me she had decided to go to her daughter.

After one and one-half days on the train, she arrived, but she was shocked to learn that the doctor had sent her daughter home from the hospital. He had said there was nothing more they could do. They had used radium; it was too late to operate, and there were other complications. He told the patient she was going to die.

My neighbor, the little mother, told me she was surprised to hear herself saying to the daughter: "My dear, you do not have to die, no matter what they tell you, so do not give up. My friends in Unity are praying for you, and you and I will pray together." At first the daughter clung to the thought that she had to die. But after a few hours, the mother sensed a change. Every hour showed improvement.

Three days later the doctor ordered the daughter back to the hospital for surgery. The surgery took about three and one-half hours. A few hours after the operation, the doctor visited the patient. He said, "I am amazed; I do not pretend to know what has happened. You had a decided cancerous condition of the lower intestines. The x-rays showed a mass too. During the surgery, my assistant and I looked over every inch of the intestines carefully. We found no cancer, no inflammation, not even irritation. It is a miracle!"

The delighted patient said she knew what had happened. The prayers her mother's friends had been saying for her and the family's prayers had been answered.

My little neighbor has just returned home, having been away for two weeks. Her daughter was laughing and chatting with her friends when the mother left her. She was preparing to leave the hospital.

The mother said she could never be grateful enough for the help given. She herself was still up in the clouds. It was all so wonderful—the healing, her own strength, and the remarkable change in the whole family.

—M.I.

∼

Several years ago I was hospitalized for two months with bleeding ulcers. They were so bad that the doctors said I was not going to recover. As a final resort, they were going to operate but said it was hopeless. My aunt called Silent Unity for prayer. The next day the surgeons took x-rays for the operation and could not believe what they saw. The x-rays showed nothing—they were perfectly clear—not even any scar tissues remained.

I am alive today because of prayer. Thank you.

—D.T., OHIO

As we see from the testimonials, medical professionals often are at a loss to explain such miracles. Their patients who know the power of prayer know the answer.

⌒⌒◯⌒⌒

I want to thank Silent Unity for their prayers and concern for my nephew, who is 15 years old.

He had been told by two doctors that he had cancer. I called Silent Unity to join me in prayer for God's healing hand to be with him.

When the surgeon began to operate, God—the master of all surgeons—had already been there. The results were negative. I thank God for his recovery.

—*P.C.*, INDIANA

Healing Addictions

Addictions are one of the most serious health issues faced by individuals and by society. Addictions exact a terrible toll on personal health, on relationships, and on our ability to function in the world. Conquering an addiction can be one of life's greatest challenges. Prayer helps us find the resolve to do it.

⌒⌒◯⌒⌒

Thank you is so inadequate to express the fullness of my heart for all at Unity and in particular Silent Unity. Since I phoned you in utter desperation and misery, it having just dawned on me that I am an alcoholic, nothing but good has happened to me.

The most important happening is that I was prompted to get in touch with AA. I was lodged there almost immediately. I remained there nine weeks and three days, and I thank God for such a place. When I consider how few of those who succumb to this powerful drug, alcohol, ever recover or seek help, I shudder and pray that God in His infinite goodness and mercy will be able to use me to convey by my life, or I should say by Christ life in me, the good news of salvation from this drug.

The relationships with my family are now a joy. Understanding, sympathy, helpfulness, and love abound. I am growing up, maturing, and my friends have rallied round. My cup runneth over.

I was strengthened as I joined with you and others in prayer at set times. I clung to the conviction that prayer was being offered and God was hearing and answering. And so it was and is. Bless you, dear Silent Unity.

—R.O.M., CALIFORNIA

Low self-esteem is often at the root of addictions. Myrtle Fillmore taught that the first step in healing addictions is to surrender all grief, worry, condemnation and censure, whether directed at one's self or at others. Surrender these negatives and allow a picture of divine perfection as part of God's plan to fill the mind. "It is up to you to accept your God-given perfection for yourself, put aside the past mistakes and the untrue suggestions, and fix your undivided attention upon the Creator of your inner pattern of perfection," said Myrtle. "This is the secret of success in all spiritual treatments. You must bring all of your mental attitudes, the centers of your consciousness, and even your physical structures, to this high place in Divine Mind where you see as God sees."[6]

When a person is in the grip of addiction, life begins to shrink. Self-esteem slides, and the tasks of daily living become increasingly daunting. The world grows narrower and darker, until it seems there is no hope. A single prayer, however, can turn the situation around and bring the light of God to where there is darkness.

Unity has helped me realize and overcome the habits and temptations that were weighing me down. It has made me see the things that I was doing to myself and to my family. I lost faith in God. I became afraid of my own shadow. I didn't want anyone to come into my home, to visit me or my family. For weeks at a time I wouldn't go out of the house. I would get all kinds of anxiety attacks. Everything I did was a major task for me. The simplest things were put off. I would tell myself, "I will do them tomorrow," but I would never get around to doing them.

I stopped reading Unity material because it revealed things about myself that I didn't want to see. I am so glad for the morning I prayed and asked God to help me to overcome an addiction to alcohol.

I thank God every day for letting me rise alcohol-free. I am sending this letter and praising God and my Unity family for all that has been done for me and my family.

—A.H., Illinois

~

At the time I asked my wife to call Silent Unity for prayers, my life was uncontrollable and undesirable. I was lost and hopeless. I had been using alcohol most of my life (thirty years) and it had gotten to the point where it ruled my life. I had tried to stop drinking many times but found that it was impossible.

While sitting at the bar, feeling very alone, I felt a tap on my right shoulder, and I was asked if I had had enough. I turned to answer, but the bar was empty except for the bartender and me. I set my glass down and went for treatment for alcoholism.

I know that I have a long and hard road ahead of me, but as long as I keep in sight that God is with me and with the power of prayer, my life will come back to order.

—J.C., Illinois

Once we accept our perfection and our oneness with God, we can receive divine healing. "Let the same divine love of God which Jesus described in His story of the prodigal son fill mind and heart and flow out to all concerned," Myrtle said. "When we love, and pour out the subtle love essence which stirs the heart center, we are moving to action the life energies of Being, and a great law of mind equilibrium is fulfilled. . . . So, let us go to the Source of all help, all life, all supply, and all opportunity, and build up the consciousness of health and plenty. Instead of struggling in an outer way, let us go within and build a foundation for real success and prosperity and satisfaction."[7]

Thank you for your help and prayers these past few weeks. I cannot tell you how much they have helped me. I have lost completely the desire to smoke cigarettes. I am quite grateful, but the feeling for which I am most thankful is that of being free from an overwhelming sense of fear—no specific fear—just an unknown dread I carried around with me all the time. I think the fear was caused mostly by the fact that our children are now grown up and married and many miles away from us. I lost sight of the fact that they are never out of God's hands, even if I cannot be near them.

I have been studying Truth for some time, but I needed your prayers to give me a little help in the right direction. Thank you, and I will try to stay on the right beam now that I am started.

Enclosed is a check to help with your wonderful work, and may God bless all of you. I am going to continue saving the money I formerly spent on cigarettes and send it from time to time to help with the Unity work. I am sure it will do great good used in that way, to further God's Truth. I am so very grateful to be free of the cigarette habit. Sending my offerings will be a constant reminder that you are always there for me to call on and will help me so that I shall not fall into the same bad habit again.

—P.M.S.

I called you some time ago when my husband was detoxifying from methadone, a drug substitute for heroin. I was overcome with stress as I tried to handle our business alone.

The voice on the phone lifted my spirits by reminding me that my work was a service for God. Immediately, I received help and guidance. I was able to hire someone who was keeping a day free because she "had a feeling" she would be needed even though she could have worked somewhere else.

Truly, God had answered my prayer before I asked.

My husband is now completely free of drugs and seeing a counselor to help him remain free. I bless all my clients and thank God for being able to serve them.

It's a new day and a new life. There is hope, there is love, and there is a light that shines in my life through Unity.

God bless you! I love you!

—M.B., New Jersey

Prayer helps us manage all situations in life. After healing—prosperity, abundance, and success draw a large number of prayer requests. Prayer helps us see our path clearly and get our priorities straight.

Chapter Seven

Prosperity and Abundance in Life

There is no need to suffer lack. God provides unlimited prosperity and abundance. When we are attuned to God, we see this great abundance and we bring it into manifestation.

What is real prosperity? Too often, we equate prosperity with money piled up in the bank. True prosperity is living in accordance with divine love. When our hearts are filled with divine love, we set things right on the spiritual plane, which in turn sets things right on the material plane.

———————

I phoned requesting your prayers that some sales which were about to be lost to my husband might be completed. I am happy to say that the largest one was somewhat ingeniously completed, and we are extremely happy and grateful for the speedy answer to your and our prayers.

Thank you for all your help, and please continue to pray for us as there is much more involved than money in my husband's succeeding in this new work. I hope to keep his morale high and to make other people happy who need his services, since he is a highly trained and very honest man.

—W.W.S., Colorado

～

Our affairs are looking more prosperous than they have for years. You told me that my confidence would be rewarded. Those were words of Truth. My eyes are opened to the wonderful Truth of Life. I have had a wonderful uplift. Harmony is being restored in my home, and I give thanks and rejoice continually.

—A.A.F., Washington

Through divine love, we banish fear. It is fear that breeds poverty, among other ills. Fear creates a fertile ground for worries and negative thoughts to take hold, and thus generates the very conditions of lack that we seek to escape. Fear creates resentments, judgments, attachments, and a "debt mentality" that leaves us constantly checking the ledger book of life.

Recently I wrote to you asking you to pray that I would get a job that was suitable for me. I had applied to many places in regard to obtaining a job. I had job interviews at some of these places; I was even offered three separate jobs, but these just didn't seem to be suitable. My final interview was last Friday, and I was supposed to find out this Friday if I would get the job. This job seemed to be the suitable one, but the lady had two other people to interview.

Well, tonight I was reading your booklet Formulas for Health, Happiness and Success, *and I was reading the part about fear being a great breeder of poverty. (Tonight I was also becoming somewhat concerned about my upcoming bills.) I started reading the part that says if you talk about poverty and lack in the home, you are making a comfortable place for these unwelcome guests. I then started to affirm that I would obtain the job I was seeking to counteract the thoughts of poverty and lack. At the time I was affirming this to myself, the phone rang and it was the lady informing me that I could have the job if I was still interested!*

I couldn't believe what a coincidence this was—but, as some say, there really aren't coincidences!

—*K.W.,* Kentucky

∾

I would like to express my heartfelt appreciation for the prayers and support of Silent Unity.

After months of only part-time work and being 55 years old, my husband was getting desperate. I called you for help and, after praying with you, I felt completely at peace. I never doubted again.

To make a long story short, my husband started a new job 16 days after my call to you. God bless you all.

—*B.A.,* Wyoming

∾

I was notified that I was to be audited by the IRS. Although I have been honest in my dealings with the IRS, I was nonetheless frightened because people always say how frightening the IRS is to work with. I am disabled, and the prospect of going through an audit caused a lot of stress. The auditor that had been assigned to me had already been very rude, and this caused even more stress.

I called Silent Unity and asked for help. My accountant and I put all the necessary records together and went to the IRS. When we arrived, we were informed that we had been reassigned to a different auditor. Throughout the entire audit, a feeling of peace and calm prevailed. At the conclusion, she told me that I owed no additional money and wished me happy holidays.

Thank you for this and the many other times that you have been there for me.

—S.M., CALIFORNIA

"Tell me what kind of thoughts you are holding about yourself and your neighbors, and I can tell you just what you may expect in the way of health, finances, and harmony in your home," said Charles Fillmore.[1] When we forgive ourselves and others, when we love ourselves and others, and when we have faith that our unlimited good can be obtained, we manifest true prosperity. We find the right job, the right home. We have enough money to take care of our needs. We have the family we desire. We are happy in our relationships, and we meet whatever tests and challenges come our way. Most important, we are close to God and allow the living love of God to flow through us in all that we do and all that we bring into creation.

⤳⋙⋘⤶

It has been two months since our lovely daughter was born.

I wrote to you at the very beginning of my pregnancy asking for your prayers and maternity lessons. I had had two children pass on and two miscarriages, and I was very apprehensive, but wanted a child very much.

During the months that passed, I found an inner peace that I did not believe existed. I felt assured that, through my daily meditations, my pregnancy was healthy and our child would be perfect. So many people came to me, telling me how absolutely wonderful I looked. Surely this was my inner joy reflected, a joy which would have been impossible without your guidance, love, and prayers.

Our beautiful baby was born amidst loving and faith-filled people after a joyous, easy labor, as I knew it would be.

Bless you for being there and for your wonderful teachings.

—*M.J.D.*, New York

~

I am writing this letter to thank you for helping me through three trying years.

When I was seventeen, I was having problems with my parents and my social life. I was ready to drop out of school, when

I met one of the nicest ladies in the world. She told me about Silent Unity, and I called many times for prayers.

I graduated from high school and enlisted in the Marine Corps. Today I am a proud Lance Corporal and plan on making the Marine Corps my career.

I owe all this to you, to a very special lady, and most of all, to God. Thank you and God bless you.

—B.G.N., CALIFORNIA

The Fillmores were well acquainted with lack and plenty. "There was a time when my husband was sick and without funds," said Myrtle. "You would not have seen anything in that early environment and life of ours to give peace and happiness. We didn't know where we were to get our food or clothes or money to pay our debts. There was no evidence of plenty or prosperity. We didn't have anyone to pray for us or to offer suggestions of Truth; these things we had to find ourselves, in the heart of God. . . . But we got well and helped others to get well. We found that God had ways to provide for our needs."[2]

The Fillmores believed that too much emphasis is placed upon money as proof of prosperity, when actually it is but a symbol. True wealth consists of character, spiritual ability, and the ability to bless others. When these qualities are demonstrated, the law of prosperity is fulfilled. Prosperity, said Myrtle, does not come to us but *through* us.

Calling you during a very difficult time in my life was the best thing I ever did in my spiritual search. Many good things have happened in my life during the past thirty days: I found a new job, I have a lovely roommate, I have made new friends, and I have begun to remove the paralyzing depression and negative beliefs I had fallen into over the past several years.

I am consciously dedicating time for prayer and meditation. I am keeping a special journal of the things I am grateful for.

I am working on forgiving myself and others who I perceive have been hurtful toward me.

I am renewing my active ability to heal my body and not just cope with its pain and limitation.

I am beginning to expect and believe in positive events, not just somehow waiting for the next disaster to befall me.

Knowing that your prayers were with me has been a source of great comfort and encouragement. Please keep me in your prayers for continued spiritual faith and peace of mind and healing.

—S.S., California

∼

I am healed of the poverty plague. Of this I am sure. The suffering I have had in mind all these years has been maddening, but now it is gone and there is a great peace.

—Mrs. G.B.E., Washington

Prosperity consciousness is established by eliminating negative thoughts concerning lack. This builds a positive atmosphere. We affirm our abundance, no matter what we have. If our wallet is empty, we deny the lack and affirm that we are filled with the bounty of God. Knowing that words have great power to set forces in motion, we allow no words of poverty to limit us.

"Do not say that money is scarce; the very statement will scare money away from you," said Charles. "Do not say that times are hard with you; the very words will tighten your purse strings until Omnipotence itself cannot slip a dime into it. Begin now to talk plenty, think plenty, and give thanks for plenty."[3]

True thanksgiving is like rain falling upon ready soil: it nourishes the growth of prosperity itself. "Let praise and joy and blessing fill your mind, body and affairs," said Myrtle. "... Bless those whom you owe and those who owe you.... There is nothing like appreciation, love, praise and thanksgiving to increase your good. The more you praise and give thanks, the greater will be the outpouring of the riches of the kingdom."[4]

I am so thankful to write that I see God's bountiful supply manifested. The strain and stress from without is being removed, and I am more at peace. Everything looks brighter, and I am truly thankful.

—Mrs. J.A.C., Texas

Thank you so much for all the prayers for employment you have offered for me and my husband during the summer.

Not only did I call asking for employment, but the "right" employment in a position where I would not become bored and unhappy as I had been in several temporary jobs.

I am now working for a manufacturing company, which is busy, active, and challenging. Not only has my request been granted, but my husband and I both have a new business venture ahead of us in which we will be able to reach goals, dreams, and the financial security for our family that we have always wanted. God truly has many good things in store for those who love Him!

Words cannot express my heartfelt gratitude to Silent Unity for your prayers and to God for His wonderful answers.

—C.B., OREGON

When we find ourselves in lack instead of in receipt of our good, we can right our course through prayer.

For the past ten months I was trying to find a job. Many were the days when I was worried and depressed but my faith in God and his love kept me going. On many occasions I turned to Silent Unity to pray for me and just knowing that you were praying along with me helped me to keep searching and not lose hope.

God has answered our prayers. Finally, I have a job and it is just what I needed. I am truly happy and grateful to the Lord for my job. I thank you all for your prayers. To God be the glory. I praise Him and thank Him daily for all that He has done in my life. May He bless you richly.

—Y.C., NEW YORK

∼

Our affairs are looking more prosperous than they have for years.

I called for prayer for my husband on the day that he had a job interview. He had not had a steady job for five years. I am very happy to say that my husband got the job.

Thank you very much for your prayers, and special thanks to the Prayer Room worker who took my call and prayed with me at that hour.

—M.R., New York

∼

A little over a month ago I wrote to Unity asking help for employment.

I had been unemployed for practically one year after working at one place for 12 years.

About two days after receiving your letter I obtained what I think is the best position I have ever had.

The staff appears to be very friendly and the atmosphere is wonderful.

—J.D., California

As we saw in Chapter 4, effective prayer requires being open to all possibilities for a resolution. True prosperity consciousness rests in the assurance that God provides for our needs. We should never doubt that there exists a way to solve a problem.

Recently I wrote you asking your prayers for a very desperate need I had for financial aid. A day or two later I again wrote you with a request for the Secret of Unlimited Supply—*which I received last night and I am very grateful to you for that.*

The next Friday I left work for a week's vacation, still with all the unpaid bills and really not too much to look forward to in the way of peace of mind. As I wrote you in my letter, even though I had no idea how I could ever get the help I needed, I still hoped and prayed.

On that same night I received a phone call, saying that I was to receive a sum of money which I never expected, and from a completely unexpected source. Even while I was taking the message on the phone, my prayer of thanks was going to God— and to all who had helped me. The amount was not a fortune, believe me; but just to be able to take care of the very necessary bills, and to have peace of mind for a while, was greater than a fortune! I honestly believe that my receiving the money just when I did was nothing short of a miracle. It had to be. I am sure now that God never fails.

The amount enclosed is to say, "Thank you." Please continue to pray for me and my needs, as I do for others. And I pray that my faith will never leave me. My prayers of thanks go to all of you.

—L.H., MASSACHUSETTS

Prosperity in life concerns more than just making money. It is our success in any endeavor. Prosperity is measured in many ways, including our ability to experience joy in life itself.

I called and you prayed with me for a job interview the next day. Well, all is in divine order—they hired me on the spot! I am now doing my heart's desire and using my God-given talents full-time and making a good living. Praise God and bless you all.

—S.G., MASSACHUSETTS

Many prayer requests are made to Silent Unity for successful school and professional examinations.

Enclosed you will find a donation to Silent Unity as a token of my thanks for prayers answered.

I recently took the [state] bar examination and throughout my studying I came to a mental block several times. Each of those times I called the Silent Unity prayer line and received the most inspirational prayers. I know that these prayers subsequently helped me through my studying and the exam itself. It restored my confidence and upon walking into the exam I said an extra prayer. When the exam was over, I felt pretty confident that I had passed the exam.

Then there was the 2½ months. Well, I found out last week

that I did pass the examination. I continued to pray with my Daily Word *and knew everything would work out. All good things work together for those who love the Lord.*

Therefore, I just want to say thank you to Silent Unity for their continuous prayers.

—*A.M.,* New York

∼

A few weeks ago I called you to ask for your prayers for my granddaughter, E— . She is a student of pharmacy at the [university]. As part of her requirement to graduate, she must serve an apprenticeship with a druggist. The students are expected to get their own apprenticeships.

E— wrote countless letters and went to many interviews. She had no success, I called you for prayerful assistance. I am grateful to tell you that this week E— has received a fine apprenticeship. She and all of us are so very grateful.

—*B.G.,* Oregon

∼

Recently I telephoned Silent Unity and requested prayer for my son who was having a bad time in school with his studies.

I am delighted to report that within two short days he showed marked improvement in both his class and homework studies! He now brings home A's.

When I told him that I requested prayers for him, he didn't believe that strangers would pray for him. He even thought God didn't care about the hard time that he was going through. He now believes that prayer does change things! My deep and sincere thanks to all of you lovely, unselfish people at Unity Village for the prayers that you are praying on behalf of my beloved son.

—J.H., California

I called to ask for prayers for our son who is beginning a course in electronics. His fear of failure was so great that he was not able to concentrate. He is the oldest member in the class.

That evening when he returned, he was jubilant. Everything had gone very well for him, and he is steadily gaining the confidence he needs to go on.

It is truly wonderful to know you can receive help in your prayers when at times you seem overwhelmed by unbelief.

—D.E., Pennsylvania

For many others, prosperity is selling a house quickly to enable a move or finding just the right home.

Some weeks ago I wrote asking for prayers for the sale of my daughter's home. Thank you for your help. God guided the right person to the house, and it was sold.

A happy family left here for a new home and job in Chicago, and I thank God and you for your prayers which, along with mine, made this move possible. I cannot put into words the love and thanks I have for all you have done.

　　　　　　　　　　　　　　　　　　　—E.B., MINNESOTA

～

Many are the times I've called Silent Unity requesting prayer for healing, prosperity, my two sons, etc. Always have I received loving support and care. Recently, I called as I needed to find a place to live. I'm on a fixed income, and my choices appeared to be few.

At about the midnight hour, I saw an ad in the paper for an A-frame house (loft bedroom). I went to see it, and the moment I walked in it felt right.

And it was affordable. When I talked to the realtor, she told me someone else was also interested, and she would let me know. I talked to her later, and she had taken a deposit. I felt let down because I had had the feeling it was the right place for me.

It doesn't end here. The next day I received a call, "The A-frame is yours if you're still interested." I was elated! I'm experiencing an answer to collective prayer, and I thank all of you from the bottom of my heart.

　　　　　　　　　　　　　　　　　—K.L.W., NORTH CAROLINA

～

About two weeks after we asked for your help, we sold half of our ranch and have fair promises of selling the remainder in the near future. The party that bought it seems so happy and contented. We know without a doubt that it was through your help that we were able to sell, for we had tried for a number of months before without success. We also have had a great spiritual uplift that means more than all else. We are so happy and thankful for all our blessings.

—D.M.A., CALIFORNIA

∼

God bless you dedicated people. Throughout the years you have supported me in prayer.

Thank you for your assistance in the sale of my home. It sold after only sixty days on the market. Since real estate is selling slowly right now, it was a wonderful surprise.

Thank you for your loving support.

—D.R., NORTH CAROLINA

Prosperity also includes restoration of that which is ours—possessions which are lost or stolen. Losing something essential or precious, such as money to pay the bills or family treasures, can fill us with sorrow, anxiety, and even panic. However, nothing is ever truly lost to us if we place ourselves in God's hands. Prayer restores a calm mind and strengthens the faith that what is ours shall be returned to us.

I called Silent Unity because my purse was missing. A calm, serene voice answered my call and told me, "In God's world nothing is missing. Your own will return to you." I felt better after hearing this, and felt a peace inside me that helped me truly believe my purse would be returned to me.

Two hours later, I got a call from a man who said, "Are you missing something?" This man had found my purse in the middle of a busy boulevard. He gave it back to me intact!

Praise the Lord! Thank you so very much for your prayers and help. God is so wonderful.

—K.A.F., Washington

I am writing to thank you for your prayers and to share a wonderful testimony!

My husband lost his wallet, along with all his credit cards, keys, his monthly train pass, money, and his work admission pass. We had planned an outing, but losing the wallet caused such confusion that we canceled it.

I called my friends at Silent Unity and asked for help. A few hours later the police rang our door bell to return the wallet—with all contents intact! A woman had found it and turned it in to the police.

Only God could move miraculously through all things to get action like this. Thank you for your prayers and for standing with us in faith when we needed it most.

—P.M., Illinois

〜

Last Sunday I called and asked you to pray for my son. His car, with all of his clothes in it, had been stolen. On the following Monday he called to tell me that the car and all of the clothes had been found. I immediately gave thanks to the Lord and I thank you for praying with me. Very truly yours,

—A.D., Tennessee

When something is lost, we must not despair of having it returned—and returned intact—even when time passes with no results or others tell us to expect the worst.

One week ago I walked outside to find that my car had been stolen. After calling the police, I called Silent Unity for help and prayers. The woman who talked with me was wonderful and helpful. I felt very calm and peaceful during the following week and kept my faith, despite hearing from many sources who said I wouldn't receive my car back or that it would be damaged. As a result, yesterday—one week after it was taken—my car was found a few miles away, totally intact, with no damage

*whatsoever! I am grateful to God and to all of you at Silent Unity
for your help and support.*

—S.S., Oregon

∽

*On Friday June 9, while I was traveling on a train between S—
and G—, I lost my wallet. This morning it was returned to me with
the contents intact, including money, driver's license, membership
cards, and personal treasures such as snapshots of dear friends,
which cannot be replaced. More than half of the money belonged
to my father, who can afford the loss even less than I.*

*My friends and relatives shook their heads mournfully when
they learned of the loss, and I began to despair myself after
inquiring at all possible stations on the railroad and being told that
the wallet had not been turned in.*

But one good friend, a subscriber for Unity, *said, "Don't believe
that you have lost it. Hold on to the faith that it will be returned
with everything in it." And almost every day, she said, "I'm still
holding the faith that our wallet will be returned intact." Although
I know nothing of the teachings of Unity, it was easy for me to
accept this philosophy, for I have always had a strong faith in the
honesty and kindheartedness of people, a faith that has seldom
been violated in my experience.*

*Yesterday I was informed that my belongings had been turned
in at the N— terminal by a member of the train crew, and this
morning they were returned to me by messenger. I have no idea*

why this railroad employee delayed so long in returning my property, and I have no wish to know. All I know is that his innate goodness made it possible for my loss to be retrieved.

When I learned that my things were on the way back to me, I decided to make some contribution to Unity to show my gratitude for the faith that made this good fortune possible. My check is enclosed for your use in any way you see fit in forwarding your good work. I wish the check could be for a great deal more.

—S.A.B.

Prosperity is ours when we keep ourselves centered on God. Prayer also brings us into the true prosperity of the heart, made possible when we learn the lessons of love and forgiveness.

Chapter Eight

The Miracle of Love and Forgiveness

    Sometimes our greatest pain comes not from illness or adversity but from difficulties in our relationships with others, especially those whom we love. In counseling and praying with others about relationships, the Fillmores always kept the focus on the highest purpose of life—to glorify God. When we follow that purpose, we are naturally guided in the right direction, whether it means letting go of a relationship or taking on a new relationship.

⌦⌫

I've been praying with you for a little over a year now, and for the first time in my life I can say, enthusiastically, that I'm a happy person! I ended my participation in an alcoholic relationship with no leftover feelings of bitterness. Somehow my situation at work has improved; I no longer hate my job. Relationships have developed and improved, and I am able to appreciate the many pleasurable aspects of my life. These are all things that, try as I might, I was never able to affect.

You showed me a way of understanding life. There's a sense of satisfaction in seeing things from the perspective that you suggest. It brings an inner glow that never gets extinguished. From the first time I read **Daily Word** *I knew this was what had been missing in my previous religious experience. I knew your philosophy was right. The study of Truth has enabled me to let go and let God. You have certainly let Him express through you, and I bless you for all your prayers and insights.*

—J.H., PENNSYLVANIA

〜

I must tell you of all the good things that have come to us. If I had never heard of Unity, today I might have been groping in darkness and worry as before. But, thank God, you have taught me how to live, how to think, how to speak and how to feel, until all things are working together for good. Our family are now united, and we had been separated for two years. We are all happy and try to worship God every day in every way. I also have had wonderful success in securing work, and I now have a permanent position at a good salary. I shall always praise and give thanks for the many blessings I have enjoyed in the past year, and for the success in the business world. I am alive in Christ forevermore.

—T.S., TENNESSEE

Glorifying God is simple: it means filling every thought, word, and deed with love. The more we do this, the more we become continuous fountains of refreshing, loving energy. Our outlooks change, our behavior changes—and others are positively affected as well.

You have helped me with your prayers for years, and I love and bless you for always being there when I write or call. I have appealed to you not only for myself but for others, and always there has been a healing—whether it is physical, mental, or emotional.

During the past year I wrote about a serious breach between myself and my dearest and oldest friend. I wrote later to ask for your prayers regarding my marriage—wanting a renewal or rejuvenation.

The results have been miraculous. It came from within myself—a new awareness and greater insight. It literally flooded me with love, and we know that love heals all. I see the world with new eyes. God bless you!

—*E.L.*, OHIO

For quite some time now, I have been trying to get over a very painful relationship, and in my quiet loneliness and despair, I called Silent Unity. Your prayers gave me the strength and courage to meet the challenge of my loneliness and reminded me that indeed I am not alone. God is with me always, and I feel God's presence and love. Now I have a new, special friend in my life and know not what the future holds—simply taking things one day at a time is a blessing. However, I had been delivered from the pain of the loneliness and find life very peaceful and rewarding.

I called Silent Unity about a job where I might be a blessing to the company and they to me. That prayer has been answered and now I have a wonderful job that grows more special each and every day.

—D.B., TEXAS

⟨⟩

Upon receiving your letter informing me that I had become a link in a powerful chain of prayer that encircles the world, I have truly been blessed.

My request for prayer involved my divorce. I needed strength and guidance. I am happy to tell you that my husband and I have gotten back together and the love between us is stronger than ever.

I know that prayer is most powerful, and he and I are continuing to pray together, believing.

—S.B., OHIO

Wounds from troubled relationships often cannot heal until we forgive. When we forgive, we experience a tremendous healing of body, mind, and spirit. It matters not whether we are forgiving a fresh wound or an old hurt; the liberating effect of divine goodness is the same. Forgiveness is central to the teachings of Jesus, who taught us in the Lord's Prayer to ask God to "forgive us our debts, as we also have forgiven our debtors" (Mt. 6:12). Jesus also told us to "love your enemies, do good to those who hate you, bless those who curse you, pray for those who abuse you." (Lk. 6:27-28).

Sometimes we are truly and deeply wronged. Sometimes we prefer to believe we are wronged when, in fact, we share a good part of the blame for a situation gone awry. No matter who's to blame, resentments and grudges only hold us captive to a spiritual darkness. We cannot truly heal until we learn to forgive. In forgiving, we put ourselves in harmony with the Truth of Being and all transgressions are eliminated. We are filled with the unconditional, healing love of God. Our forgiveness may not change the other person, but it does change us in profound ways. There is no limit to the healing power of forgiveness, as Jesus illustrated when he told Peter to forgive "seventy times seven" (Mt. 18:22 RSV).

Myrtle Fillmore advised: "When the harshness of others seems to crush you, you can send forth love, the power that not only blesses you but goes forth to redeem the adverse conditions in the outer. When petals of the fragrant rose are crushed by cruel hands they send forth their sweetness even more than before. 'Love therefore is the fulfillment of the law' (Rom. 13:10 ASV). The law of God in your heart keeps you sweet always."[1]

Not long after entering chiropractic school, my relationship with my fiancee exploded, and I found myself in an ugly lawsuit. It tore me open emotionally. I knew when I entered chiropractic school that I would have to face all of my personal demons, but I never realized that one of them would be something this extreme. The woman that I had spent five-and-a-half years with was now part of a machine that was designed to grind my life up and spit it out.

About four or five weeks after my relationship blew up, I was still very traumatized and much in need of healing. I attended a seminar to learn the second level of Reiki healing. It involved a series of initiations that each student went through individually with the instructor.

During one of the initiations, I was seated with my eyes closed, and the instructor was in front of me, praying. I took a deep breath and my head fell back as I felt a spiritual presence. A surge of energy shot up my spine, and chills went through me. I realized that Jesus was with me! I had feelings of unworthiness because of the recent events in my life, but on another level I knew that I was worthy of his presence. Tears of gratefulness and joy flowed down my cheeks.

As I let go of my fear and apprehension about what was going to happen in my life, he moved closer to me, like someone coming to embrace me from behind. Then he literally moved into my body. He was merged with me. I was sobbing with joy. There was such a feeling of release, forgiveness and reaffirmation of who I was: as a human being, as a healer, as someone who has done much spiritual work in this lifetime, as someone who deserves to be able to continue to live his life's purpose. All this came at once, these feelings of knowingness that I was going to be all right.

My Reiki teacher remained in front of me. She had the wisdom to witness what was going on. She could feel a powerful energy coming out of my heart. After a few minutes, I felt Jesus start to move back from me and upwards.

Afterwards, I felt washed and lighter in essence. Whatever was unclean or would impede the flow of healing energy in my life had just vanished. I can still feel the power of it. Even in recounting the story, I'm sweating, as I did then. When I left the initiation, my shirt was soaked.

Jesus left me with several messages. The main message was that everything was going to be all right. My divine mission in life and my opportunity to give my gifts as a healer would be protected. Another message had to do with forgiveness. When you don't forgive, the person you injure the most is yourself.

—*C.M.,* Missouri

Forgiving ourselves is just as important as forgiving others. We are often harsh on ourselves, holding ourselves accountable for mistakes long past done and gone. "When you forgive yourself, you cease doing the thing that you ought not to do," said Charles Fillmore.[2]

Thank you for praying for me. Your prayers have moved me through months of turmoil.

I was full of self-righteous, self-centered hate. I hated myself. I couldn't accept my past actions, words and deeds. I didn't, or couldn't, forgive myself. And I continued making the same mistakes over and over again, blaming other people for the wrong choices I made. I finally ran out of blame; I ran out of people.

I am an alcoholic, and when I saw the turmoil that my wife and sons had experienced because of me, it was enough. I admitted my wrongs to another human being and to God. Today, the weight of hate has lifted. I see through "new eyes."

Through prayer, both my ex-wife and I have moved closer to God. Thank you, Unity.

—A.W.K., TEXAS

Forgiveness does not mean being "soft and without backbone and individual conviction," said Myrtle, who counseled some abused spouses to end their marriages. "Forgiveness is not silent consent, the negative appearance of making the best of a situation while underneath there is resentment. Forgiveness is the art of putting something else in place of the thing forgiven. You put the positive realization of the Truth of Being in place of the appearance of negation and adversity which your senses and your intellectual training report."[3] Thus forgiveness is a demonstration of spiritual strength. We replace negative emotions with love.

I want to share a miracle with you. One year ago I had a cranioaneurysm and was expected to live only twenty-four hours. Instead I was in the hospital three months. I have had multiple sclerosis for over twenty years, and the doctors do not know how I survived the aneurysm.

When I came home from the hospital, depression and fear set in. Part of the fear was because of my landlady. While I was still in the hospital, she came to see me and told me she did not want me back at the home I rented from her because she was afraid I would get sick again and she and her husband would have to care for me. My heart and friends were there so I did go home.

When weakness and depression set in again, I telephoned a friend who suggested I call Unity. The woman who answered the telephone prayed for me. She asked me if I was holding any animosity. I realized that I was holding animosity toward my landlady. When I realized that she was fearful at having me there, I changed my thinking from animosity to love for her. I was kind to her and today we are good friends and she does all she can to help me.

Your prayers pointed out my animosity and changed my thinking and brought about love. I want to get stronger and completely well so I can help others. I have come so much closer to God. I could tell you of many blessings of love and caring from so many people, and I want to manifest God in every way.

Thank you for helping me that night, and for the good that comes every day. Please pray for me to throw away my crutches and do God's will.

—M.J.S., OREGON

We should not be concerned about obtaining immediate results from our forgiveness, Myrtle believed. "It does not matter that there is no immediate transformation; you have made use of your God power to erase the appearance and to establish Truth. Such an attitude invites only the best from other souls.

"If it does not seem that justice is meted out to you, you must know that there is no hindrance to infinite justice. Whether you realize it or not, you may be holding on to the thought that a wrong was done. Your own thoughts and ways must change to conform to the divine plan and law, in which justice is a quality and an active reality. Light of divine understanding and love will show you that no wrong was intended, and no wrong done. You will see the whole matter in a different light, and so your whole being will be flooded with a great love—even gratitude for the good that is to come as a result of the experience of the past."[4]

———

I want to thank you for your recent help in praying with me and for me.

Last week I was going to court for what could have been a very bitter divorce trial. After two years of ugliness, the divorce was finally granted very peacefully. Not every issue was settled favorably for my daughters and me, but those that weren't, we can find other answers to.

I truly believe that the more people praying together for a specific problem, the better the outcome. The kind voice at the other end of the phone was a blessing.

I know that there is nothing that prayer cannot help, and I have learned through all this that good comes from all situations. Your kindness and concern are very much appreciated.

—*D.K.*, Missouri

———

We can progress a long way toward wholeness and unity with God by learning to forgive instantly. By coming to terms immediately with adverse thoughts and feelings, we release them before they have a chance to take hold in our consciousness.

Chapter Nine

When the Elements Rage

When disaster strikes—when the elements unleash a fury—prayer brings salvation and relief. As callers and correspondents testify, many people credit prayer with surviving disasters and sustaining little or no harm. Facing the destructive forces of nature tests our powers of faith and will: we must have faith in divine protection, and we must align our will with the harmony of the universe.

Jesus gave his disciples a lesson about faith when he calmed stormy sea waters (Mk. 4:35-41). After teaching parables all day to a large crowd by the sea, Jesus and his disciples departed in a boat. A great storm arose and began to fill the boat with water. Jesus remained asleep in the stern, but his disciples became greatly alarmed. They awakened him and said, "Teacher, do you not care that we are perishing?" Jesus awoke and rebuked the wind and said to the sea, "Peace! Be still!" The wind died down, and the waters became calm. Jesus turned to his disciples and said: "Why are you afraid? Have you still no faith?"

When the elements rage, we become fearful. Faith is an antidote to fear. Through prayer, we establish and proclaim our faith and rest in the assurance that all will be well. We come out of such an experience with our faith stronger than ever.

∽≈≈∽

God is constantly present, protecting, guiding, and assuring us even when flood waters threaten and assail us. God's loving, restoring power was demonstrated to us in our experience and the experience of many others who were threatened and suffered loss during the destructive flood which swept through Denver on June 16.

My husband and I were alerted to the danger of the flood about 5:30 that evening by a neighbor of his aunt, both of whom lived near the Platte River in the path of the waters. We hurried to his aunt's home, some three miles distant, and met some difficulty from the police who insisted that the area had already been evacuated. We felt quite sure our aunt would not leave voluntarily, as it had been her home for 58 years, and she had promised her husband she would never leave the place during her lifetime.

Although 80 years of age, she was at this time out taking drivers' training lessons, and while we were trying to gain admittance to her home she drove up in a training car. She was indignant when my husband told her we had been looking for her.

When the serious situation was explained, she became calm but in no mood to leave her home. Only after several hours of argument would she gather together several articles to take with her. As we closed the door, all the lights in the area went out. We waded through water ankle-deep first, then it rose quickly, and before we could reach higher ground we were in it shoulder-deep.

The pickup, which we had to leave, was by now completely covered.

My husband was practically carrying his aunt, and I had her belongings and our purses. Some men on a roof heard our voices and directed us to one of their homes out of the danger area. We were provided with dry clothing and coffee and were housed during the night in a small camp trailer in their yard. We did not sleep, but were able to relax. I had discovered the loss of my purse, but so much gratitude for our safety filled our hearts that this seemed a small loss. We were so grateful for these good people who had befriended us and that we had escaped the flood waters.

Several days later I received a call from a woman whose son had found my purse. He thought at first it was a box sticking up out of the ground, but upon cleaning it discovered my purse. The woman mentioned some money in the coin purse, but did not mention the $100 tucked away in another compartment which was still there intact. The boy was not permitted to accept a reward as his mother said she wanted him to learn one must help others without expecting pay. Our pickup was damaged, but we were able to secure another.

Out of this experience has come a deeper faith in God and His goodness, and in the many people who were so generous with their help and hospitality. It has increased our awareness that we are all God's children, united in a bond of trust, respect, and brotherliness. I am grateful for the Unity teachings and for the

Unity Truth center here in Denver. I feel that greater blessings have been restored to us than those which seemingly were lost.

—*N.E.A.* Colorado

Faith sets in motion a great spiritual force like electricity, declared Charles Fillmore. "There is a button in the mind of man that connects him, through faith, with almighty energy. . . . It is not necessary that the one who touches the button of faith shall understand all the intricate machinery with which he makes contact; he knows, like one who turns the electric switch, that the light or power will spring forth."[1] Experiences with this spiritual force quicken the consciousness, said Fillmore, and build the transforming power of the mind.

I want to thank you for your prayers through a recent hurricane. It was headed our way, but turned and went out east, so we just got rain. I thank God and all of you folks.

—*F.G.,* Massachusetts

Here is a love offering for your Prayer Room. I called for help when a storm was approaching our area. Well, the storm never did take place in this area. We were surprised, for the wind was really bad for a while, but it soon died down. Your prayers were answered quickly, and my sister and I were overjoyed at the peace all around us. We are so grateful and thankful to God, and all in the Prayer Room. Bless you all, all is well again. Our prayers were answered so quickly. Many thanks for the Prayer Room workers, and bless them always. Sincerely and lovingly,

—G.A.R., FLORIDA

Through prayer, we also invoke the power of will. The true use of will is not imposing or forcing our desires, but aligning our desires with the will of God. Charles termed will, as we usually use it, "the negative pole of the great executive force of the universe."[2] Prayer and meditation open the will to this tremendous force, whose power "reaches into the invisible realm of ideas and controls the elements."[3] When we align our will with divine will, we achieve a unity with the forces of nature. We cannot be harmed by that with which we are in perfect harmony.

Thank you so very much for your prayers during the Hurricane Andrew ordeal!

I called for prayers on Sunday for my parents and sister who live in C— and K—. As you know, these areas were hit very hard. Miraculously, their homes were spared. Huge trees missed their home by inches, and trees fell all around *their car—not on top. As the storm whipped about their home, they surely felt the protecting power of God. I had given them "The Prayer for Protection." Through the night they affirmed it again and again.*

The hurricane was devastating beyond belief, but it taught us many things. Among these—we are blessed. Thank you for your special support!

—S.H., FLORIDA

Sometimes we must keep praying and affirming our will. The Old Testament prophet Elijah prayed for rain in order to end a severe drought and famine and to demonstrate that the Lord, not Baal, ruled the heavens (1 Kings 18:41-46). Elijah climbed to the top of Mt. Carmel and began praying. After a while, he sent his servant to look toward the sea to see if any rain clouds were forming. There was nothing in the sky. Elijah kept praying. Six times he dispatched his servant, only to be told that no rain was in sight. On the seventh try, the servant reported a tiny cloud about the size of a man's hand. Soon the sky was filled with black clouds, and a torrent of rain fell to earth.

Elijah's lesson is that if we truly believe in God's power, we do not give up when there are not immediate signs.

As I prepared to leave my home to seek safer shelter from Hurricane Andrew, I didn't know if I would have anything to come back to. My neighbor and I stood at our doors, and I said, "It will be a miracle if we are spared from this deadly storm." Before I locked my door, I called Silent Unity for prayers for divine order in the weather and all things.

My niece and her family had just gone through the terrible ordeal and their homes were spared, and now it was my turn. All through that long and frightening night, I held to the truth that divine order was in progress and that we would be fine—and we were! It gave me great peace to know that Silent Unity was there praying for us.

We, in this city, know how blessed we are. We ask that you continue to pray for strength and courage for those who fell victim to the ravages of this horrendous disaster, and I thank you with all my heart for being there.

—C.W., LOUISIANA

～

In the Sierra Mountains we had had several days of extremely high winds, rain, and snow. I felt the power might go out, so I began preparing kerosene lamps, getting out wool blankets, etc. I also felt a strong urge to add an affirmation card on divine love and order in weather conditions. The power went out as the winds increased. Warmly tucked into bed, I silently repeated my weather affirmation, and I felt a great calm. At midnight, we heard a crash. The next morning we discovered a huge pine had snapped off. The tree fell across three lots, missing six houses and tool sheds. A neighbor came over and said he couldn't have planned such a perfect fall for that tree if he had been cutting it down. I just smiled to myself and thanked God for his loving presence during the storm. Love,

—M.K., NEVADA

Many times people call Silent Unity to ask for safety and protection before they set out on a trip. Whether it's a two-hour drive or a trip of several days, the energy of prayer provides a buffer against accidents, crime, illness—and even the unexpected turns of weather.

Earlier this year, before beginning a vacation to Nevada, I phoned the telephone Prayer Room and requested prayers for a safe journey. My husband and I left shortly thereafter, feeling safe and reassured. After approximately thirty minutes of driving, we turned on the car radio and, for the first time in our lives, heard a warning signal followed by the radio announcer's voice—"This is not a test, this is a tornado warning!" Tornadoes had been reported on the ground, and people in the town through which we were to travel were told to take cover.

The tornado must have passed just in front or just behind us as we passed through the town. We were blessed and safe. We never had to leave our car or take cover.

Thank you for your prayers and your wonderful and blessed work.

—C. & D.M., KANSAS

Prayers that affect the forces of nature sometimes seem more surprising to us than those that bring medical miracles. Perhaps this is because we tend to see nature as apart from ourselves, acting on its own accord. Prayer teaches us the unity of all things, the oneness of all creation. Prayer puts us into a high, positive state of consciousness that truly enables anything to be possible.

Chapter Ten

God Cares for Animals Too

Pets are part of the family, as treasured as the humans who share the household with us. Their unconditional love buoys us when we feel low. Their companionship brings us great pleasure and fills lonely spaces. A sick or lost pet can cause just as much distress or grief as misfortune befalling a family member or dear friend. When a problem with a beloved pet arises, the right thing to do is to turn to God in prayer.

~~~~~~~~~~

About two weeks ago, I saw my cat hit by a car, and then he just disappeared, and we couldn't find him. It was the coldest and wettest of weather. Shortly after midnight I called Silent Unity because I just didn't want him to suffer out there some place.

I had my doubts about asking for prayers for a cat, but the lady that answered assured me that God looks after His little creatures too and I needed to turn it over to Him.

Two days later, P. appeared at my back door, frightened, bewildered and hungry, but all in one piece. After several days of TLC, he is now feeling fine, but is afraid to go outdoors. Perhaps that is good.

I appreciate the prayers of Silent Unity, but especially I want to thank the lovely lady who helped me to get some sleep that night and strengthened my faith in what "let go and let God" is all about.

I thank Silent Unity for coming to my aid once again. God bless you all.

—S.R., CALIFORNIA

∼

This letter is to let you know that prayers are indeed answered and that I am grateful for your help and concern.

On December 27, my husband and I each called you separately asking for prayer for our dog J. who was hit by a falling display unit in a pet-food store and, in his blind panic, broke the leash and ran out the store into traffic.

My heart was full of terror as I saw him running through six busy lanes of traffic. I immediately asked God for a miracle and started an all-night search for our terrified pet. Neither I nor my husband could sleep.

The two calls to Silent Unity did help to calm our frayed nerves. The voice on the line was both confident and soothing. And, of course, we had many friends praying for us and helping with our search.

Thank you, God, for answering our prayers! A kind-hearted woman saw J. in the middle of a busy city street many miles away from the accident. She and her husband rescued him and took him to the animal shelter.

Some people may say I'm foolish to pray for a lost dog, but I believe all of God's creatures are precious, and all of them deserve our love and care. Thank you, Silent Unity, for your prayers. God does indeed work miracles!

—R.C., Florida

～

I called in January and was comforted by the interest and concern of the Silent Unity worker I spoke with. I'm happy to say that my cat M. returned home safely after four days in a blizzard! God works miracles in many ways, and I'm always grateful for Silent Unity when my faith wavers or my emotions take control.

—K.R., Tennessee

Animals benefit from prayer just as do humans. They, too, need divine healing, comfort, protection, and care. Our duty to be loving and compassionate to all creatures is expressed in this anonymous prayer:

"O Lord Jesus Christ, Who hast taught us that without our Father in heaven no sparrow falls to the ground, help us to be very kind to all animals and to our pets. May we remember that Thou wilt one day ask us if we have been good to them. Bless us as we take care of them. For Thy sake. Amen."[1]

Every Sunday the first column I turn to in Weekly Unity *is "Silent Unity." As one continues to work with the Silent Unity workers, one always feels as though the "Silent Unity" column is our article or letter from home.*

I am enclosing a love offering. Use it as usual to help others help themselves by being open, and receptive, to the articles they receive; and I bless the offering and the ones who receive it.

I have a cute little dog. She is a Pekingese, and she had a growth at the corner of her eye. Well, I'd read to her and tell her she was God's little dog—an idea of love. Honestly, to see her attention one could say she knew what was going on. I told her divine love removed everything that was offensive and cleansed every channel and healed perfectly always.

After a week, the growth dropped off. It was the size of a pea; and as I cleansed the eye she was a very good little patient and a very happy one.

—B.W., FLORIDA

∼

I would like to express my thanks to you. I phoned you in regard to my beloved pet, F. After we spoke, I experienced a calmness and a surrender to the trust of God's care for my dog. She was seriously ill. I phoned the following morning to check on her, and the vet said she was showing signs of improvement.

I picked her up three days later and brought her home. She is back to her old self. Thank you so much.

—K.S., CALIFORNIA

～

I just wanted to thank you for your prayer help. Last week I called your prayer line about a lost dog named B. I was very anxious because I left her behind when she turned up at the place I work. I left work hoping she would "find her way" home. I could not bring her home because I have four dogs and feared my husband would be upset.

The Prayer Room worker I spoke with was very understanding. I felt very comforted when she reminded me that God was watching out for B. and for me when I made my decision. I continued to help look for B. but felt assured that God was watching over her. Two days later I received a message at work that she had been found around the time we were saying a prayer for her. Thank you so much.

—C.H., NEW YORK

Epilogue

In the preceding pages, we've seen dramatic examples of how prayer works in specific situations. Many people find a much broader and greater effect of prayer. In addition to helping the resolution of challenges, prayer ripples out to affect everything in life for the better. Many letter writers echo the sentiments expressed in these testimonials:

I have been wonderfully helped physically and mentally; my finances, too, are looking brighter. I am more grateful than I can express for this new life. I have never read anything that gave me more pleasure than your literature, and I am learning more and more how to trust God and his Divine guidance.

—S.E.A., INDIANA

Thank you so much for your prayers and guidance over the telephone. Last summer I had ripped ligaments and other problems in the knee. The surgeons said there was no way it would heal, and I would need an operation. I called you and I prayed, and now I can walk long distances and ride horses and do many other things.

In the past you have helped me so much with a positive attitude that situations would turn out well despite bad appearances, and things have turned out so well in my life that it is even happier than I could have imagined.

I hope God will use me as one of his instruments to help others. I work in a doctor's office, so I am blessed with an opportunity to express God's love and to help patients by being positive and cheerful.

Thank you again for your prayers.

—*K.T.*, CALIFORNIA

Our discovery of the power of prayer often is made out of need to resolve a difficulty. We apply prayer to the situation and obtain results. We find we can adjust any condition in life. But the power of prayer does not end there. The high purpose of prayer is to help us discover God. The more we engage in prayer, the deeper our prayer becomes and the more profound effect it has on life and on spiritual growth.

Instead of praying solely for things, we begin to pray more for knowledge and for the strength and wisdom to use knowledge rightly. Our vision changes from the material to the spiritual. The more we elevate our consciousness through prayer, the richer the message we receive from God in answer.

"Our most effective prayers are those in which we rise above all consciousness of time and space," said Charles Fillmore. "In this state of mind we automatically contact the spirit of God. Indeed when we elevate our consciousness to that of Jesus Christ, the God presence becomes as meaningful to us as it was to Him. It is in this state of at-one-ment that we truly become aware of His sublimity and power."[1]

Prayer awakens us to our role as cocreators with God. Like K.T., we seek opportunities to be channels for the expression of God's love. Prayer liberates our greatest gifts. This wonderful journey begins with just a few moments of turning inward and turning toward divine light.

Notes

Works by Charles and Myrtle Fillmore frequently cited are identified by the following abbreviations:

TT   Charles Fillmore, *Talks on Truth,* Unity Village, Mo.: Unity School of Christianity, 1926.

TPM _____, *The Twelve Powers of Man,* Unity Village, Mo.: Unity School of Christianity, 1930.

P_____, *Prosperity,* Unity Village, Mo.: Unity School of Christianity, 1936.

JCH_____, *Jesus Christ Heals,* Unity Village, Mo.: Unity School of Christianity, 1939.

ASP_____, *Atom-Smashing Power of Mind,* Unity Village, Mo.: Unity School of Christianity, 1949.

KTL_____, *Keep a True Lent,* Unity Village, Mo.: Unity School of Christianity, 1953.

TTP   Charles Fillmore and Cora, *Teach Us to Pray,* Unity Village, Mo.: Unity School of Christianity, 1941.

HL   Myrtle Fillmore, *Myrtle Fillmore's Healing Letters,* Edited by Frances W. Foulks, Unity Village, Mo.: Unity School of Christianity, 1948. Originally published as *Letters of Myrtle Fillmore.*

HLG_____, *How to Let God Help You,* Selected and arranged by Warren Meyer, Unity Village, Mo.: Unity School of Christianity, 1956.

Introduction

1. *The Miracle of Prayer: True Stories of Blessed Healings,* New York: Pocket Books, 1995.
2. The dream of an angel over Unity Village at sunset appears to have come true in the photograph used on the cover of this book. The dream and the photograph, *Angel Over Unity Village, Mo.,* by Myra M. Cox, came about independently of each other, but the photograph is a serendipitous

and apropos discovery for the cover. Cox took the photograph on August 12, 1983, after attending a talk at Unity Village. She was photographing a beautifully colored sunset (such as seen in the dream). When viewing her slides later, Cox saw the angel.

3. Testimonials make reference to *Unity, Daily Word,* and *Weekly Unity. Unity Magazine* and *Daily Word* are monthly publications of Unity School of Christianity. *Weekly Unity* is no longer in publication.

Chapter One *The Light That Shines for You*
1. Vahle, p. 109.
2. Witherspoon, pp. 41–43.
3. *ASP,* p. 133.
4. Vahle, p. 10.
5. Interview with author, April 1996.
6. Freeman, p. 211.
7. *Ibid.,* p. 212.
8. Interview with author, April 1996.

Chapter Two *In the Twinkling of an Eye*
1. *ASP,* p. 126.

Chapter Three *Prayer That Works*
1. *JCH,* p. 59.
2. *Ibid.,* p. 98.
3. *HLG,* p. 76.
4. Vahle, p. 60.
5. *Ibid.,* p. 61.
6. *KTL,* p. 142.
7. Vahle, p. 69.
8. *TTP,* p. 17.
9. *HL,* p. 20.

10. *Ibid.*, p. 18.
11. *TTP*, p. 20.
12. *JCH*, p. 76.
13. Vahle, p. 62.
14. *JCH*, pp. 82–83.

Chapter Four *How to Pray*
  1. *TTP*, p. 45.
  2. *HL*, p. 18.

Chapter Five *All Prayers Are Answered*
  1. *ASP*, p. 126.
  2. *JCH*, p. 85.
  3. *Ibid.*, pp. 124–125.

Chapter Six *Healing Body, Mind, and Soul*
  1. *TTP*, p. 31.
  2. *JCH*, p. 80.
  3. *HL*, p. 44.
  4. Vahle, p. 27.
  5. *Ibid.*, p. 61.
  6. *HLG*, p. 135.
  7. *Ibid.*, p. 99.

Chapter Seven *Prosperity and Abundance in Life*
  1. *P*, p. 118.
  2. *HLG*, p. 150.
  3. *P*, pp. 103–104.
  4. Vahle, p. 69.

Chapter Eight *The Miracle of Love and Forgiveness*
1. *HLG*, p. 105.
2. *JCH*, pp. 58–59.
3. *HLG*, pp. 66–67.
4. *Ibid.*, p. 67.

Chapter Nine *When the Elements Rage*
1. *TPM*, p. 31.
2. *Ibid.*, p. 108.
3. *Ibid.*

Chapter Ten *God Cares for Animals Too*
1. Guiley, *Blessings*, p. 198.

Epilogue
1. *TTP*, p. 12.

Bibliography

Fillmore, Charles, *Talks on Truth*, Unity Village, Mo.: Unity School of Christianity, 1926.

———, *The Twelve Powers of Man*, Unity Village, Mo.: Unity School of Christianity, 1930.

———, *Prosperity*, Unity Village, Mo.: Unity School of Christianity, 1936.

———, *Jesus Christ Heals*, Unity Village, Mo.: Unity School of Christianity, 1939.

———, *Atom-Smashing Power of Mind*, Unity Village, Mo.: Unity School of Christianity, 1949.

———, *Keep a True Lent*, Unity Village, Mo.: Unity School of Christianity, 1953.

Fillmore, Charles and Cora, *Teach Us to Pray*, Unity Village, Mo.: Unity School of Christianity, 1941.

Fillmore, Myrtle, *Myrtle Fillmore's Healing Letters*, Edited by Frances W. Foulks, Unity Village, Mo.: Unity School of Christianity, 1948. Originally published as *The Letters of Myrtle Fillmore*.

Fillmore, Myrtle, *How to Let God Help You*, Selected and arranged by Warren Meyer, Unity Village, Mo.: Unity School of Christianity, 1956.

Freeman, James Dillet, *The Story of Unity*, Unity Village, Mo.: Unity School of Christianity, 1978.

Guiley, Rosemary Ellen, *The Miracle of Prayer: True Stories of Blessed Healings*, New York: Pocket Books, 1995.

———, *Blessings: Prayers for the Home and Family*, New York: Pocket Books, 1996.

Unity: 100 Years of Faith & Vision, Unity Village, Mo.: Unity School of Christianity, 1988.

Vahle, Neal, *Torch-Bearer to Light the Way: The Life of Myrtle Fillmore,* Mill Valley, Calif.: Open View Press, 1996.

Witherspoon, Thomas E., *Myrtle Fillmore: Mother of Unity,* Unity Village, Mo.: Unity School of Christianity, 1977.

About the Author

Rosemary Ellen Guiley writes and lectures on spirituality, consciousness, and exceptional human experience and potential. She is the best-selling author of numerous books including three other explorations of the power of prayer: *The Miracle of Prayer: True Stories of Blessed Healings, Blessings: Prayers for the Home and Family,* and *Wellness: Prayers for Comfort and Healing.* She also has authored encyclopedias of dreams and angels. Her works have been translated into twelve languages and published around the world.

Ms. Guiley, who has studied and practiced various forms of healing and meditation, has been featured on The Discovery Channel, The Learning Channel, and in the *Time-Life* video series. She serves on the board of trustees of the Academy of Religion and Psychical Research, the academic affiliate of the Spiritual Frontiers Fellowship International, and is an Honorary Fellow of the College of Human Sciences, the professional membership division of the International Institute of Integral Human Sciences in Montreal, a nonprofit organization affiliated with the United Nations.

If you have prayer needs,
write: **Silent Unity**
1901 NW Blue Parkway
Unity Village, MO 64065-0001
or call: (816)969-2000
On-line: http://www.silentunity.org